FISHER V. YANKEE DOODLE CORPORATION

Problems and Case File

NATIONAL INSTITUTE FOR TRIAL ADVOCACY

Educational Services Committee

1993 – 1994

FISHER V. YANKEE DOODLE CORPORATION

Problems and Case File

C. Steven Fury
Attorney at Law
Seattle, Washington

FOURTH EDITION
1993

NATIONAL INSTITUTE FOR TRIAL ADVOCACY

Fury, C. Steven, *Fisher v. Yankee Doodle Corporation Problems and Case File* (Fourth Edition, 1993).

ISBN 1-55681-381-3

09/93

Section I

Problems

FISHER v. YANKEE DOODLE CORPORATION

Problems

Table of Contents

INTRODUCTION

The problems in this book are intended to simulate realistic courtroom situations. Advance preparation is essential to their successful utilization as instructional materials.

All years in these materials are stated in the following form:

- YR-0 indicates the actual year in which you are trying the case (that is, the present year);

- YR-1 indicates the next preceding year (please use the actual year);

- YR-2 indicates the second preceding year (please use the actual year); etc.

DIRECT, CROSS, AND REDIRECT EXAMINATION

The ability to examine and oppose the examination of witnesses in open court in an adversary setting is the most basic skill of the trial lawyer. Yet, the most common criticism of trial lawyers is that they are unable to conduct proper, intelligent, and purposeful examinations and to oppose these examinations.

As with any skill, practice is the only sure way to achievement. The practice should be conducted with some guidelines in mind.

1.   The purpose of any witness examination is to elicit information.

2.   The basic format is an interrogative dialogue.

3.   The witness is probably insecure. She is appearing in a strange environment and is expected to perform under strange rules. This is a handicap you must overcome on direct and an advantage you have (and may choose to exploit) on cross.

4.   Your questions should be short, simple, and understandable to the witness, the judge, and the jury on both direct and cross examination.

   (a)   It is imperative that your audience — the judge and the jury — understand your question so that they can reasonably anticipate and comprehend the answer.

   (b)   On direct examination, the insecurity or anxieties of the witness will be increased if he does not understand your questions.

   (c)   On cross examination, the complex argumentative question provides a refuge for the witness to evade the point.

5.   As a general proposition, you may not lead on direct except as to preliminary matters or to refresh the recollection of the witness. Both of these exceptions are discretionary with the judge.

6.   In any event, on direct examination leading questions and the perfunctory answers they elicit are not persuasive.

7.   On cross examination you may lead and you should do so. Control of the witness on cross is imperative.

8.   At the outset of direct examination, have the witness introduce herself. Then, place her in the controversy on trial, and elicit the "who, where, when, what how, and why" of the relevant information the witness has to offer. Then quit. Do not be repetitious.

9.   If you know that the cross examination will elicit unfavorable information, consider the possible advantage of eliciting it during your direct examination.

10. Do not conduct a cross examination that does nothing other than afford the witness an opportunity to repeat his direct testimony.

   (a) If there is nothing to be gained by cross examination, waive it.

   (b) If you can accomplish something by cross examination, get to it. Organize your points and make them.

   (c) Be cautious about cross examining on testimony elicited on direct that was favorable to your position. You may lose it.

   (d) Be cautious about asking questions to which you do not know or cannot reasonably anticipate the answer. Be particularly cautious in these situations if the only evidence on the point will be the unknown answer.

11. Listen to (do not assume) the answers of the witness. As an examiner, you are entitled to responsive answers. Insist on them by a gentle repetitive question on direct or a motion to strike on cross. Of course, if the answer is favorable, accept it and return to the pending question.

12. Objections to the form of the question must be made before an answer is given. If the question reveals that the answer sought will be inadmissible, an objection must precede the answer. The grounds of the objection should be succinctly and specifically stated. If the question does not reveal the potential inadmissibility of the answer, but the answer is inadmissible, a prompt motion to strike should be succinctly and specifically stated. Only the interrogator is entitled to move to strike an answer on the *sole* ground that it was unresponsive to the question. If the answer is unresponsive *and* contains objectionable matter, then the opposing counsel is entitled to object.

13. If an objection to the content of the answer (e.g., relevancy, hearsay, etc.) as opposed to the form of the question, is sustained, then the interrogator should consider the need for an offer of proof at the first available opportunity. If an objection to the form of the question is sustained, then the interrogator should rephrase the question to cure the objection.

PROBLEM 1

Julie Fisher

Assume the case is at trial and the plaintiff's first witness is Julie Fisher.

    (a)   For the plaintiff, conduct a direct examination of Ms. Fisher.

    (b)   For the defendant, conduct a cross examination of Ms. Fisher.

    (c)   For the plaintiff, conduct any necessary redirect examination.

PROBLEM 2

Dr. Brian McBride

Assume the case is at trial and the plaintiff has already called Julie Fisher as a witness. The plaintiff's next witness is Dr. Brian McBride, M.D.

    (a)   For the plaintiff, conduct a direct examination of Dr. McBride, concentrating on the issue of damages.

    (b)   For the defendant, conduct a cross examination of Dr. McBride, concentrating on the issue of damages.

    (c)   For the plaintiff, conduct any necessary redirect examination.

PROBLEM 3

Roger Mitchell

Assume the case is at trial and the defendant's first witness is Roger Mitchell.

    a)   For the defendant, conduct a direct examination of Roger Mitchell.

    b)   For the plaintiff, conduct a cross examination of Roger Mitchell.

    c)   For the defendant, conduct any necessary redirect examination.

Fisher Problems

HANDLING AND INTRODUCTION OF EXHIBITS

The ability to examine and oppose the examination of witnesses in open court in an adversary setting is the *most basic* skill of the trial lawyer.

The second basic skill of the trial lawyer is the proper, efficient and orderly handling and introduction of tangible evidence. Again, however, a common criticism of the trial bar is its lack of facility in this truly simple undertaking.

This is all the more regrettable when one considers the highly persuasive quality of relevant exhibits. Jurors (and judges, too) trust them. They are the real thing. They do not exaggerate as witnesses do and they do not overstep their bounds as lawyers do. Many a case has been won or lost because a particularly intriguing exhibit was received in evidence or excluded.

The four touchstones for the handling and introduction of exhibits are:

1. Authenticity
2. Relevance
3. The Hearsay Rule
4. The Best Evidence Rule

These four touchstones must be satisfied before an exhibit can be received in evidence. Some call it "laying the foundation." By whatever phrase, the essential element is testimony establishing that the exhibit is authentic and relevant and complies with both the hearsay and best evidence rules.

Authenticity is simply a demonstration that the exhibit is what it purports to be. Is this thing — whatever it is — that is being offered in evidence, *prima facie* that which it purports to be?[*] The essential requirement is testimonial vouching for the thing unless, of course, authenticity is established by admissions in the pleadings, discovery, or a request to admit. See, for example, Federal Rule of Civil Procedure 36.

Relevance, as well as the hearsay and best evidence rules, is intrinsically dependent on the issues raised in the case and the purpose for which the exhibit is offered in evidence. In each instance, however, the foundation must be laid demonstrating that the exhibit is relevant and that it complies with the hearsay and best evidence rules.

For each exhibit, counsel should check the four touchstones and then lay the foundation necessary for its admission in evidence through the testimony of one or more witnesses.

As in the case of witness examination, the skill of handling and introducing exhibits is developed by practice and is conducted with certain guidelines in mind.

1. Select with care the witness or witnesses you will use to lay the foundation for your exhibits. A mistake here could be fatal.

---

[*]The standard is a *prima facie* showing of authenticity, as the court determines admissibility. The weight to be assigned to the particular piece of evidence is left to the fact-finder.

2. Because the introduction of exhibits usually is done through witnesses, keep in mind the basic principles of witness examination.

3. Have the exhibit marked for identification by the appropriate court official (usually the court reporter or clerk) at the earliest opportunity. Many lawyers have their exhibits marked for identification prior to trial in the sequence in which they expect to use them. Some judges insist on this. It is a good practice in cases involving many exhibits. But also consider the advantages to be gained from a brief pause (respite for the witness) and a little bit of the lawyer doing his or her "thing" that attends your stepping to the bench and requesting in a voice the jury can hear, "Your Honor, may the reporter mark this document (or object) defendant's exhibit 1 for identification?"

4. Once the exhibit has been marked for identification, include that identification in any reference you make to the exhibit and see to it that your opponent, the witnesses, and the judge do likewise. Never permit the record to read merely, "this letter" or "that bottle" or "the photograph," etc.

5. Proceed to "lay the foundation" as follows:

   (a) Elicit from the authenticating witness those facts that qualify him or her to authenticate the exhibit. For example, have the witness say he saw the gun in the robber's hand.

   (b) Have the witness identify the exhibit by saying, for example, that State's Exhibit 1 is the gun (or looks like the gun) the witness saw in the robber's hand.

   (c) If the condition of the exhibit is a factor in its relevancy, either elicit testimony that its condition has not changed between the event and the time of trial, or offer a testimonial explanation of the change in condition.

   (d) If the exhibit is a reproduction of a place, a thing or an event (e.g., a photograph or a tape recording), elicit testimony that it fairly and accurately portrays that which it purports to portray.

   (e) If more than one witness is required to authenticate or connect the exhibit, withhold your offer until you have completed your foundation. A premature offer and rejection can condition a judge to reject the exhibit later when the foundation has been completed.

6. Once the foundation for an exhibit has been laid properly, offer it in evidence and obtain a ruling on its admissibility. In some jurisdictions an exhibit may not be offered during cross examination, and in those instances the formal offer of the exhibit is reserved to your case in chief or rebuttal.

7. When you are opposing the introduction of an exhibit, you are entitled to conduct a cross examination on the foundation before the court rules on the offer. The scope of this cross examination, often referred to as a voir dire on the exhibit, is limited to the admissibility of the exhibit. The proponent of the exhibit should be alert to so limit the voir dire on the exhibit and not permit the opponent to conduct a general cross examination on the weight that is to be given to the exhibit.

8. When you are opposing the introduction of exhibits, be on the alert for changed conditions and distortions (particularly in photographs). Insist that an adequate testimonial explanation of the changes be given by the authenticating witness.

9.   Do not permit your opponent to display tangible items in the presence of the jury until they are marked for identification and proffered to the witness for identification.

10.   Keep a separate record of the status of your exhibits and those of your opponent. Know at all times their identification numbers, their general descriptions, the witness or witnesses who authenticated them, and whether they have been offered and received or excluded. Many lawyers keep a columnar record somewhat like this:

Plaintiff's Exhibits

No.	Description	Witness	Date or page of record offered	Date or page of record received	Date or page of record refused
1.	Letter from Jones	Smith	6/1/88 p. 138	6/1/88 p. 140	
2.	Hammer	Jones	6/2/88 p. 100		6/2/88 p. 210

11.   At the close of your case, if you are uncertain as to the status of any of your exhibits, re-offer them before you rest.

Each exhibit has its own standards of authenticity and admissibility. For our purposes, they are better demonstrated than described.

PROBLEM 4

Photograph

Assume the case is at trial.

a) For the plaintiff, introduce into evidence the photograph marked plaintiff's exhibit 1. You may use any witness(es) you desire to lay the foundation for the exhibit. Examine the witness(es) to the extent necessary to lay the foundation and then offer the exhibit. Be prepared to discuss your choice of witnesses.

b) For the defendant, oppose the examination of the witness(es) and the offer of the exhibit. Be prepared to voir dire the witness(es) on the admissibility of the exhibit.

PROBLEM 5

Diagram

Assume the case is at trial.

a) For the plaintiff, conduct a direct examination of Julie Fisher with respect to the layout of the upper level of Yankee Doodle Burgers. Use the diagram of Yankee Doodle Burgers that appears in the case file as a demonstrative aid to illustrate the witness's testimony. Prepare a diagram that is large enough to be shown to the jury.

b) For the defendant, oppose the use of the diagram as a demonstrative aid and conduct a cross examination of the witness.

IMPEACHMENT AND REHABILITATION OF WITNESSES

Impeachment

Although it is a part of the cross examiner's art, impeachment is a sufficiently difficult problem in itself to warrant separate consideration.

(a) The cross examiner must consider not only how to impeach, but also whether the witness should be impeached at all. Just as the trial lawyer should not cross examine in some situations, he often may decide wisely that, although impeaching evidence is available, it should not be used. If the witness has not hurt your case, usually it is better not to impeach and risk offending the jury. If the testimony of a witness can be turned to your advantage, as in the case of a truly impartial expert witness, do so and do not impeach.

(b) Foundation for impeachment by prior inconsistent statement:

(1) Under the law of most jurisdictions, the witness must be confronted with a prior inconsistent statement during cross examination. If his or her attention has not been called to the earlier statement, extrinsic evidence of it will not be admissible. Cross examination should be specific as to the time, circumstances, and content of the earlier statement.

(2) The rule requiring a foundation for prior inconsistent statements is relaxed under the Federal Rules of Evidence. Federal Rule 613(b) provides that the witness must be "afforded an opportunity to explain or deny" the prior inconsistent statement in order for extrinsic evidence to be admissible, but no time sequence is specified. Therefore, as long as the witness is available to explain the inconsistency if he so desires, extrinsic proof is admissible.

(3) Most advocates will prefer to lay a foundation on cross examination regardless of whether or not it is required under the rules. The reason for this is twofold. First, the witness may admit the statement, making extrinsic evidence unnecessary. More significantly, confronting a witness with her own inconsistency often will have a dramatic impact that cannot be duplicated by introducing evidence of the earlier statement through another person.

(c) If the witness denies making an earlier statement, be prepared to prove it by extrinsic evidence.

(d) If the witness admits making an inconsistent or otherwise impeaching statement, do not ask questions that give him an opportunity to explain it away, unless you are certain that this cannot be done. The attorney who has called the witness will have an opportunity on redirect examination to elicit explanations, if any are available. This affords you the opportunity for recross.

(e) There is no need, and it is usually harmful, to dwell on the impeaching matter after it has been brought out in cross examination. Remember, you have a closing argument.

Rehabilitation

If a witness has been impeached during cross examination, counsel must evaluate whether to attempt to rehabilitate the witness on redirect examination.

(a) As with any redirect examination, counsel should limit the scope of the redirect to those items in which the witness needs an opportunity to explain or amplify upon his testimony after the cross examination. Redirect examination and rehabilitation of a witness is not the time to rehash the direct testimony once again.

(b) In considering whether to rehabilitate a witness on redirect examination, counsel should first of all be absolutely certain that the witness has, in fact, been impeached. If the witness has not been effectively impeached, do not attempt to rehabilitate the witness as you may only worsen matters.

(c) Rehabilitation generally consists of providing the witness with an opportunity to explain the circumstances pertaining to the impeachment and to elicit any "exculpatory" factors. Give the witness the opportunity to put the impeachment in context.

(d) If the impeachment can be explained, do it; if not, leave it alone on redirect as you just may worsen matters.

(e) If the witness has been impeached by a prior inconsistent statement, counsel should consider the admissibility of any prior consistent statements. See 801(d)(1)(B) of the Federal Rules of Evidence. Prior consistent statements are generally admissible if they rebut an express or implied charge of recent fabrication.

PROBLEM 6

Roger Mitchell

Assume that Roger Mitchell has testified that after Julie Fisher fell, he spoke to her to be sure that she was not injured.

a)   For the plaintiff, conduct a cross examination and impeachment of Roger Mitchell.

b)   For the defendant, conduct a redirect examination to the extent it is necessary to rehabilitate the witness.

PROBLEM 7

Julie Fisher

Assume that Julie Fisher has testified that the pain in her back is constant and that her wrist continues to be a problem.

a)   For the defendant, conduct a cross examination and impeachment of Julie Fisher.

b)   For the plaintiff, conduct a redirect examination to the extent it is necessary to rehabilitate the witness.

PROBLEM 8

Merlin Lombard

Assume the case is at trial and the witness has testified in favor of Julie Fisher. You have learned that Mr. Lombard's wife owns an interest in a competing restaurant located one block away from the Yankee Doodle Restaurant where Julie Fisher had her accident. In addition, this competing restaurant is having financial problems.

a) For the defendant, conduct a cross examination and impeachment of Merlin Lombard. You may use additional evidence or witnesses for the purposes of impeachment.

b) For the plaintiff, conduct a redirect examination to the extent necessary to rehabilitate the witness.

PROBLEM 9

Dr. Rita Moran

Assume the case is at trial and the witness has testified in favor of Yankee Doodle Corporation. Assume further that Dr. Moran has appeared as an expert witness one hundred times in the past two years. In every instance, she has testified for the defense. In addition, she no longer treats patients on a regular basis, but only examines people to evaluate their injuries for insurance companies. For each examination she conducts, Dr. Moran receives a fee of $500. Each time she testifies she receives an honorarium of $1,000. In this case, she saw Julie Fisher only one time and did not speak with her treating physician.

a) For the plaintiff, conduct a cross examination and impeachment of Dr. Moran.

b) For the defendant, conduct a redirect examination to the extent necessary to rehabilitate the witness.

EXPERT WITNESSES

As a conservative estimate, eighty percent of all trials in courts of general jurisdiction involve the examination of skilled or expert witnesses. For example, in personal injury cases, there are medical experts and experts in accident reconstruction; in criminal cases, there are chemical, ballistics, fingerprint, and handwriting experts; and in commercial cases, there are economists and market analysts. The opportunities for use of skilled or expert witnesses are limited only by human knowledge and the trial lawyer's ingenuity. Accordingly, no lawyer is worthy of the name "trial lawyer" until she has mastered the techniques that attend the direct and cross examination of skilled or expert witnesses.

The function of the expert witness is to bring to the trial of a case knowledge beyond the everyday and to apply that knowledge to the facts in the case so that jurors may better determine the issues.

The basic guidelines are stated simply, but they are not so simple to apply.

1. *Qualifications.* The proposed expert witness must be qualified by training or experience in a recognized field of knowledge beyond that of the average layman.[*]

2. *Explanation of Expertise.* If the field of knowledge is at all esoteric, the expert witness should provide a brief explanation of it, particularly with reference to its application to the case at hand.

3. *Ruling on Qualifications as an Expert.* In some jurisdictions after the witness's qualifications have been elicited, the witness is tendered to the court as an expert in his or her field, and the court either accepts or rejects the witness as an expert at that time. Some courts, however, are reluctant to give their imprimatur to the witness's testimony or to rule on the witness's qualifications as an expert prior to hearing the actual opinion the expert will be asked to give. In those jurisdictions, the direct examination simply proceeds unless there is an objection, at which time the court rules.

4. *Cross Examination on Qualifications.* The opposing counsel may voir dire (cross examine) the witness on his or her qualifications at the time the witness is tendered to the court as an expert witness or, if that procedure is not utilized, before the witness is permitted to express her opinion.

5. *Basis of Opinion.* The direct examination should elicit a description of what the expert did with regard to the case and the facts that are the basis of the opinion.[**]

---

[*]Under the Federal Rules of Evidence, the test is whether the witness's knowledge, training or experience will **assist** the trier of fact in understanding the evidence or determining a fact in issue. Note also that the witness, if qualified as an expert, may testify in the form of an opinion *or otherwise.* FRE 702.

[**]In most state courts the direct examination *must* elicit the factual basis for the expert's opinion as a foundation prerequisite for the expert stating his opinion. This is the method for ensuring that the expert's opinion is based on admissible evidence.

While, in the federal courts, the underlying facts for the expert's opinion need not be disclosed on direct examination, the expert will be required to disclose them on cross examination. FRE 705. The court, however, has the discretion to require that the underlying facts be disclosed prior to the expert stating his opinion when the interest of justice so requires. *See* FRE 703.

The underlying facts for the expert's opinion are usually quite persuasive, and most trial lawyers will make them an integral part of their direct examination. The trial lawyer has the option in federal court, and she may tailor the direct examination to meet the needs of the particular case.

The facts that may be used as the basis for the expert's opinion and may be elicited on direct examination are limited to those facts that:

(a)   The expert personally observed,

(b)   Were elicited in the courtroom and heard by the expert, or

(c)   Were transmitted to him hypothetically.

In the federal courts and in some state courts, facts that were made known to the expert outside of court, and other than by his or her own perception, may also be used if they are of a type reasonably relied upon by experts in the expert's field. *See* FRE 703.

In most state courts, the hearsay rule and the other traditional principles of admissibility apply to expert testimony. Opposing counsel should keep an ear carefully tuned for the application of these principles during the expert's direct examination. In the federal courts and some state courts that have relaxed the hearsay rule and the other traditional requirements for admissibility for expert testimony, the expert may testify to, and base his opinion on, facts that are not admissible in evidence.

6.   *Opinion*. The expert's opinion may not be speculation or conjecture. Rather, it must be an opinion to a reasonable degree of certainty within the expert's field. Most courts require that the opinion be elicited in a two-question sequence: (1) Do you have an opinion as to _____?, and then (2) What is that opinion? This gives opposing counsel an opportunity to object before the opinion is heard by the jury.

When the expert's opinion is based on facts that the expert did not personally observe or hear in the courtroom, the hypothetical question format is required in most state courts. However, in the federal courts and some state courts, the hypothetical question no longer is required, and the trial lawyer has the option of using it or not. FRE 703, 705. When this format is optional, the trial lawyer's decision is a matter of trial strategy, which depends on many factors. Perhaps some of those factors will be demonstrated in the exercises.

The primary objections that are available to opposing counsel when the hypothetical question format is utilized are:

(a)   That the hypothetical question included facts not in evidence, or

(b)   That it did not include relevant facts that are in evidence.

Thus, in a complicated case the hypothetical question can be quite cumbersome. In anything but the most routine case, it can be a delicate procedure with pitfalls to snare the unwary.

7. *Cross Examination.* The expert witness may be cross examined with respect to his or her opinion on the basis of:

    (a)   The expert's qualifications,***

    (b)   Other facts in the case, or

    (c)   The published opinions of other recognized authorities in the field (learned treatises).

***The cross examination of qualifications, discussed in paragraph 4, is a *voir dire* on the admissibility of the expert's opinion. The cross examination here goes to the weight of the expert's opinion. Counsel should weigh carefully whether to cross examine in both instances or to elect one or the other.

PROBLEM 10

Merlin Lombard

Assume the case is at trial and the plaintiff has called Merlin Lombard, C.P.E. to explain his safety analysis of Yankee Doodle Restaurant.

a) For the plaintiff, conduct a direct examination of Merlin Lombard.

b) For the defendant, conduct a cross examination of Merlin Lombard.

c) For the plaintiff, conduct any necessary redirect.

PROBLEM 11

Dr. Rita Moran

Assume the case is at trial and the defendant has called Rita Moran, M.D. to explain the results of her examination of Julie Fisher.

a) For the defendant, conduct a direct examination of Dr. Moran.

b) For the plaintiff, conduct a cross examination of Dr. Moran.

c) For the defendant, conduct any necessary redirect examination.

JURY SELECTION

If one were to interview ten able trial lawyers at random with regard to how to select a jury, one would get ten different answers. The answers would range from, "Take the first twelve (or six) and put them in the box," to "Examine each juror firmly and searchingly." We will discuss the pros and cons of both attitudes as well as the way stations between.

There is virtual unanimity among trial lawyers that the makeup of the jury is important. There is also agreement among those who watch trial lawyers at work that we do a pretty fair job of jury selection, regardless of how we do it or why we excuse those who are excused.

There are certain basic guidelines that should be followed in selecting a jury:

1.   In those jurisdictions that permit the lawyers to interrogate the veniremen, realize that this is your first direct contact with the jurors. Don't alienate them. Don't try them.

2.   Know the statutory qualifications for jurors and the case law grounds for the challenge for cause.

3.   Know the number of peremptories to which you are entitled.

4.   Never challenge a juror for cause in the presence of that juror unless you have a peremptory by which you can excuse him if your challenge is overruled.

5.   Use your peremptories wisely. Do not spend them too quickly.

6.   Be alert for jurors whose background and experience indicate that they possess knowledge particularly relevant to the facts in the case. You may end up with a one-juror jury.

7.   Be alert for jurors whose background and experience indicate a high potential of prejudgment of the case adverse to your position. They may hang the jury.

8.   Seek a cross-section of the community, but bear in mind that studies have indicated a correlation between ethnic-socio-economic background and juror vote.

PROBLEM 12

Select a jury for one of the parties in the case. To permit an in-depth interrogation and analysis of each juror within a limited time frame, only four jurors will be selected. Each side will be limited to one peremptory challenge. Use the following jury information sheet.

Jury Information Sheet

Please assume the role of a person whom you know well, so you will be able to answer *voir dire* questions in that role. Please be realistic. Try to pick a role that will be commonly represented on jury panels *and not a role of an eccentric.* Your taking an eccentric role would seriously impair the realism and benefit of the exercise for your classmates, both those who serve as counsel and those who observe the exercise.

Please fill in the following form and be prepared to use it at the class session on Jury Selection. You may be asked to deliver it to the instructor in advance of the class or during the class session.

Your real name: _____

Information About You in Your Assumed Role

1.   Name: _____

2.   Age: _____

3.   Address in Nita City: _____

     (Characterize the neighborhood:) _____

4.   Length of residence in Nita City: _____

5.   Occupation: _____

     Duties in that occupation: _____

6.   Marital Status: _____

7.   Number and ages of children: _____

8.   Number of years of education: _____

9.   Other relevant information: _____

OPENING STATEMENT

The opening statement is akin to the first scene in a play — it had better capture the audience. It is the trial lawyer's first direct contact with the jury, save in those jurisdictions that permit substantial lawyer participation in the voir dire examination of the jury. Even in those states, in the overwhelming majority of cases, it is the lawyer's first opportunity to present the jury with an intelligent, cohesive description of the case.

Some trial lawyers tend to minimize the importance of an opening statement. We do not. We regard it as crucial to the successful outcome of the trial.

There is no excuse for a poor opening statement (unless, of course, the case is so poor it should not be tried). The opening statement is essentially *ex parte*; it can and should be prepared well in advance of its presentation, and it should be rehearsed.

It is a skill that can be mastered with practice more readily than any other skill. The general guidelines for opening statements are:

1. Practice, rehearse, try out, and listen to your opening statements before you make them. You have a wife, a husband, a friend, a colleague who will listen if you ask. As you rehearse, you can listen, too. The preferred audience is a lay one.

2. Recognize the opening for what it is: a prologue or synopsis of a play, a blueprint, a travel guide folder, or the old favorite — the picture on the jigsaw puzzle box. We do not urge that you use these similes when you address the jury. We do urge that you recognize the opening statement for what it is. Indeed, in conjunction with the evidentiary portion of the trial and the closing argument, it is the trial lawyer's application of the oldest of public speaking techniques: tell your audience what you are going to say, say it, and tell them what you have said.

3. Recognize the opening statement for what it is not: it is not an argument. This is not the time to infer, plead, or fulminate. It is a time to tell the jury what the case is about and what you expect your evidence will be.

4. An opening statement in behalf of the plaintiff or prosecution should include:

    (a) A request of the court and the jury: "If the court please, ladies and gentlemen of the jury."

    (b) An introduction of yourself, your client, your opponent, and his client, if not already done sufficiently during jury selection.

    (c) A cohesive, succinct, and confident summary of what your evidence will be.

    (d) A conclusion, indicating that at the close of the case you will return and request the jury to find in favor of your client.

(e) Some lawyers include the following either at the beginning or the end of the opening statement:

    (i) A brief statement of the nature of the case.

    (ii) A brief statement of the issues of the case.

    (iii) A candid acknowledgment that the burden of persuasion rests on you and the degree of the burden.

    (iv) A reading of the indictment or information (which is required in some jurisdictions).

5. An opening statement in behalf of the plaintiff or prosecution should *not* include:

(a) Reference to evidence, or which the availability or admissibility is doubtful.

(b) Anticipated defenses or defense evidence.

6. In most cases, an opening statement for a defendant should be made immediately following that of plaintiff or prosecution. If the court has granted you permission to defer your opening statement until the close of your opponent's case, be certain the jury knows this. Be very cautious about waiving a defendant's opening statement entirely.

7. An opening statement in behalf of a defendant should include:

(a) A request of the court and the jury: "If the court please, ladies and gentlemen of the jury."

(b) An introduction (or reintroduction) of yourself and your client, if not already done sufficiently during jury selection.

(c) An admonition that opening statements are not evidence.

(d) An acceptance of the issues as defined by your opponent, plus any additional ones that will be raised by the defense.

(e) A reinforcement of the principle that the burden of persuasion rests with your opponent, plus a candid recognition of any issues in respect to which it rests with you.

(f) A cohesive, succinct, and confident (but non-argumentative) reference to anticipated deficiencies in your opponent's evidence, plus a like summary of what your evidence will be.

(g) A conclusion, indicating that at the close of the case you will return and request the jury to find in favor of your client.

8. As with your counterpart, a defense counsel's opening statement should not include references to evidence of which the availability or admissibility is doubtful.

9.   Opening statements for defendant's in criminal cases often present special problems:

(a)   Never assume the burden of proving innocence.

(b)   If you have any doubt as to whether your client will testify, do not tell the jury he will. On the other hand, if you are certain he will testify, tell the jury and admonish it that it cannot fairly form any judgment in the case until it has heard from the defendant.

(c)   We would not presume to outline an opening statement in a "no defense" criminal case. Perhaps we will see one during our exercises.

10.   In criminal cases, some jurisdictions permit counsel for the defendant to reserve opening statement until the close of the state's case-in-chief. Counsel should always consider very carefully the pros and cons of reserving the opening statement until after the state's case.

PROBLEM 13

Opening Statements in Fisher v. Yankee Doodle

Present an opening statement for one of the parties in the case.

In preparing an opening statement for the plaintiff, Julie Fisher, consider how much of her medical problems to discuss before the evidence is brought forth.

Fisher Problems

CLOSING ARGUMENT

Here is the advocate in his final and finest hour! She won it with her closing argument! She was magnificent! Legion are the legends of summations.

A lawsuit is won during the trial, not at the conclusion of it. It is won by the witnesses and the exhibits and the manner in which the lawyer paces, spaces, and handles them.

The likelihood of a lawyer's snatching victory from the jaws of defeat with his or her closing argument is so slight that it hardly warrants consideration. (Compare last of the ninth multi-run, game-winning home runs; *but see* Bobby Thompson's shot heard round the world in *Giants v. Dodgers* (1951).)

On the other hand, lawsuits are lost by fumbling, stumbling, incoherent, exaggerated, vindictive closing arguments.

This is not intended to minimize the importance of the closing argument. It is merely to relegate it to its proper position, which is a summation of the evidence that has preceded it, and a relation of that evidence to the issues in the case.

Although the closing argument is not quite as controllable as is the opening statement, it is very close to it — close enough that we can say that there is no excuse for a poor closing argument.

Many trial lawyers begin to prepare their closing arguments with their first contact with the case: as the facts make their initial impressions on their minds. That is when they are as close to being jurors as they ever will be. From that first impression forward they shape and reshape their closing arguments as the facts develop. Finally they shape the trial to what they believe their strongest arguments will be; they prove their arguments.

Thus, the closing argument has a considerable impact on the trial because an able trial lawyer knows that an argument without evidence to support it is no evidence at all.

The basic guidelines for closing arguments are:

1.   Think about, prepare, and rehearse your closing argument before trial, leaving sufficient flexibility to meet the exigencies of trial.

2.   Think about, modify, and rehearse your closing argument at each break in the trial in light of the record to date.

3.   Think about, modify, and, if time permits, rehearse your closing argument at the close of the evidence and the conference on instructions.

4.   Base your closing argument on the issues, the evidence, the burden of proof in the case, and your client's right to a verdict.

5. From the standpoint of format,

    (a) Address the court, the jury, and your opponent.

    (b) Tell the jury your purpose — to summarize the facts and relate them to the issues in the case.

    (c) Make your argument.

    (d) Tell the jury what its verdict should be.

    (e) Sit down.

6. From the standpoint of delivery: do not shout, do not engage in personalities, do not tell the jury what you believe, but act and speak as though you do believe, to the depths of your soul, every word you are uttering. If you can't do the latter, don't argue.

7. As for some of the canned approaches:

    (a) Do no repeat in chronological order the testimony of each witness. Give the jury some credit; it has heard the witnesses. Put it all together.

    (b) Do not tell the jury what you say is not evidence. Why belittle your argument? The judge will do that for you.

    (c) Do not assume a burden of persuasion that is not yours.

PROBLEM 14

Closing Argument in Fisher v. Yankee Doodle

Present a closing argument for one of the parties in the case. In planning your closing, you may assume that you would have offered any or all of the admissible evidence available to your side at the trial. Assume that all of the admissible evidence available to the other party has been offered.

In many jurisdictions, counsel for the party with the burden of proof has the right to give the first closing argument and then a rebuttal argument to the defendant's closing. For the purposes of this problem, counsel for the party with the burden of proof should assume that their closing argument is the first closing argument.

Section II

Case File

FISHER v. YANKEE DOODLE CORPORATION

Case File

Table of Contents

INTRODUCTION

This is a slip and fall case in a fast-food restaurant. Julie Fisher seeks to recover damages for injuries she sustained in a fall at a restaurant owned and operated by the Yankee Doodle Corporation.

The plaintiff claims that her fall was caused by the defendant's negligence in the operation and control of its restaurant. Plaintiff asserts that the defendant was negligent in that there were inherent defects in the design and construction of the restaurant, that the restaurant was not in conformity with the Nita City Building Code, and that the restaurant was improperly maintained.

The defendant denies plaintiff's claims of negligence and asserts that plaintiff's fall was caused by her own contributory negligence. The defendant also contests the amount of damages claimed by the plaintiff.

Nita City is a large city in the State of Nita. In YR-5, Nita City passed an ordinance adopting the most recent edition of the Uniform Building Code as the law in the Nita City. The court will take judicial notice of this ordinance. The provisions of the Uniform Building Code may be proven, if necessary, by a photo copy.

The laws of the State of Nita govern the trial of this case. There is no issue of jurisdiction, venue, service of process, propriety of the parties, or ownership or control of the premises. The applicable law is contained in the proposed jury instructions that are set forth at the end of the case file.

All years in this case file are stated in the following form:

- YR-0 indicates the actual year in which you are trying the case (that is, the present year);
- YR-1 indicates the next preceding year (please use the actual year);
- YR-2 indicates the second preceding year (please use the actual year); etc.

SPECIAL INSTRUCTIONS FOR USE AS A FULL TRIAL

When this case file is used as the basis for a full trial, the following witnesses may be called by the parties:

Plaintiff:

> Julie Fisher
> Brian McBride, M.D.
> Merlin Lombard, C.P.E.

Defendant:

> Roger Mitchell
> Thomas Newburg
> Rita Moran, M.D.

A party need not call all of the persons listed as its witnesses. Any or all of the witnesses can be called by either party. However, if a witness is to be called by a party other than the one for whom he or she is listed, the party for whom the witness is listed will select and prepare the witness.

There are no other witnesses available other than those listed above. The gentleman who the plaintiff claims helped her up at the time of her fall cannot be found. Furthermore, the parties are to assume that the plaintiff's employers, if called to testify, would support the plaintiff's testimony with regard to her employment.

Required Stipulations

1. If the records custodian of the Nita City Memorial Hospital or the Macon General Hospital were called to testify, the custodian would testify that Exhibits 1, 2, 3, and 4 are business records within the meaning of the Nita Business Records Act.

2. The plaintiff did not work from December 14, YR-2, through May 1, YR-1. In May of YR-1, she earned $600 from the Ace Collection Company. From October 1, YR-1, she has earned $400 per month working for Ashley Butler.

3. The plaintiff has incurred the following medical expenses:

Brian McBride, M.D.	$ 956.00
Nita City Memorial Hospital	104.00
Macon General Hospital	2,567.32
Francis Marco, D.C.	678.00
Prescriptions	167.56
Back Brace	78.32

IN THE CIRCUIT COURT OF
DARROW COUNTY, NITA
CIVIL DIVISION

JULIE FISHER,   )
    Plaintiff,   )
)   CIVIL ACTION
    v.   )   CA 85-0172
)
YANKEE DOODLE CORPORATION,   )
    Defendant.   )

COMPLAINT

Julie Fisher, for her cause of action against defendant, Yankee Doodle Corporation, states and alleges as follows:

I

Jurisdiction is conferred upon the court by 28 N.S.A. 1332.

II

That the matter in controversy exceeds, exclusive of interests and costs, the sum of Ten Thousand and no/100 ($10,000) dollars.

III

That the plaintiff, Julie Fisher, is currently a citizen of the State of Georgia, but that at all times material to this cause of action, that she was a citizen of the State of Nita.

IV

That the defendant, Yankee Doodle Corporation, is and was at all times material, a corporation organized and created under the laws of Nita, doing business as the owner and operator of a chain of fast-food restaurants under the trade name of Yankee Doodle Burger Restaurants.

V

That the defendant, Yankee Doodle Corporation, owns and operates, and at all times material, owned and operated a Yankee Doodle Burger Restaurant located at Third and Front Streets in Nita City, Nita.

VI

That on December 14, YR-2, the Defendant, Yankee Doodle Corporation, operated and maintained its place of business at Third and Front Streets, Nita City, Nita, in a negligent and careless way in one or more of the following respects:

1. Failed to properly install and maintain handrails adjacent to the steps on the stairway from the first to second floors in violation of the Uniform Building Code of Nita, such failure being negligence *per se*;

2. Failed to properly install and maintain non-slip safety strips to the nosing of the stairs from the first to second floors, such failure resulting in an unsafe and hazardous condition;

3. Failed to move the refuse container away from near the top of the stairway from the first to the second floors, such failure resulting in the spillage of liquid so as to create an unsafe and hazardous condition;

4. Failed to install a mat or carpet in front of the refuse container, such failure resulting in the creation of a slippery condition which was unsafe and hazardous;

5. Failed to properly clean and maintain the handrail adjacent to the stairway from the first to second floors, such failure resulting in a slippery condition of the handrail so as to make it unsafe and hazardous;

6. Failed to properly clean and maintain the landing and steps on the stairway from the first to second floors, such failure resulting in a slippery condition of the landing and steps so as to make them unsafe and hazardous;

7. Failed to properly instruct cleaning personnel to clean the floor, steps, and handrail on, around, or adjacent to the stairway from the first to second floors, such failure resulting in the creation and maintenance of an unsafe and hazardous condition.

8. Failed to provide any warning of a risk of harm as to the condition of the premises or the operation thereon, such failure resulting in the creation of an unsafe and hazardous condition.

VII

That as a direct and proximate result of the negligence of the defendant enumerated in Paragraph VI and due to no fault of her own, the Plaintiff, Julie Fisher, was caused to slip, fall, and injure herself on December 14, YR-2.

VIII

That as a direct and proximate result of the negligence of the defendant enumerated in Paragraph VI, the plaintiff has been prevented and will continue to be prevented from engaging in the conduct of her profession and livelihood with subsequent loss of income, profits, and reputation all to her detriment in the amount of five hundred thousand ($500,000) dollars.

IX

That as a direct and proximate result of the negligence of the defendant enumerated in Paragraph VI, the plaintiff, Julie Fisher, was caused to suffer severe, permanent, and disabling injuries, great bodily harm, and pain and suffering all to her detriment in the amount of seven hundred and fifty thousand ($750,000) dollars.

WHEREFORE, the plaintiff, Julie Fisher, demands judgment against the defendant in the amount of one million two hundred and fifty thousand ($1,250,000) dollars, together with costs and disbursements herein and such other relief to which said plaintiff is entitled in law or equity.

Date: February 22, YR-1

Respectfully submitted,

Ronald J. Hamm

Donald J. Hamm
Attorney at Law
1600 Columbia Tower
Nita City, Nita 99993
(721) 555-0030

RETURN OF SUMMONS

I hereby certify that on February 25, YR-1 the above Complaint and Summons were personally served on Sylvia Butler.

Kathleen L. Lindley
Process Server

IN THE CIRCUIT COURT OF
DARROW COUNTY, NITA
CIVIL DIVISION

JULIE FISHER,   )
    Plaintiff,   )
)   CIVIL ACTION
    v.   )   CA 85-0172
)
YANKEE DOODLE CORPORATION   )
    Defendant.   )

ANSWER

Yankee Doodle Corporation for its answer to plaintiff, Julie Fisher's complaint, states and alleges as follows:

I

Denies each and every matter, subject or allegation except as hereinafter admitted or answered by a qualified response.

II

Admits the allegations set forth in Paragraphs IV and V.

III

That as to the allegations set forth in Paragraphs I, II, and III this answering defendant, Yankee Doodle Corporation, has insufficient information to form a belief as to the truth of those allegations and demands strict proof thereof.

IV

AFFIRMATIVE DEFENSE

That for an Affirmative Defense, defendant, Yankee Doodle Corporation, asserts that any and all injuries of the plaintiff are the result of the negligence of the plaintiff.

WHEREFORE, the defendant, Yankee Doodle Corporation, demands judgment of dismissal with prejudice of the plaintiff's pretended causes of actions, together with costs and disbursements herein.

Date: March 13, YR-1

Respectfully submitted,

Sylvia Butler

Sylvia Butler
Attorney at Law
Suite 500, Buck Tower
Nita City, Nita 99993
(721) 555-8834

Certificate of Service

I hereby certify that on March 13, YR-1, a copy of the above Answer was placed in the United States mail, postage prepaid, addressed to Donald J. Hamm, 1600 Columbia Tower, Nita City, Nita 99993.

Alice Michaelson

Alice Michaelson
Suite 500, Buck Tower
Nita City, Nita 99993

YANKEE DOODLE BURGERS
THIRD & FRONT
NITA CITY

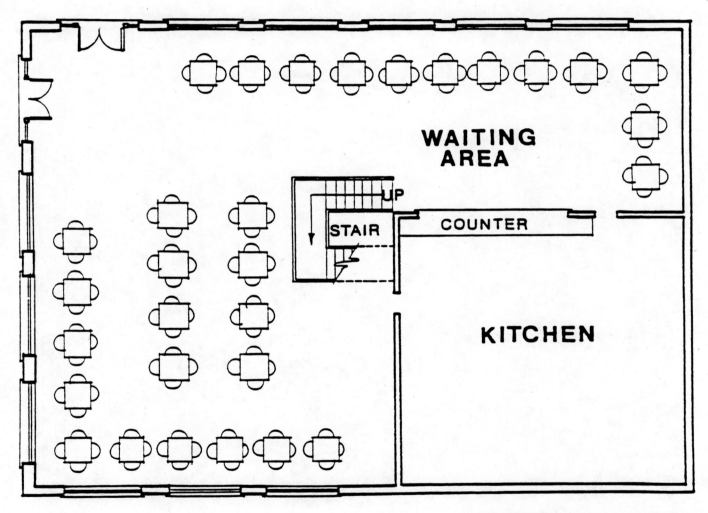

WAITING AREA

UP

STAIR

COUNTER

KITCHEN

GROUND LEVEL
NOT TO SCALE

N

YANKEE DOODLE BURGERS
THIRD & FRONT
NITA CITY

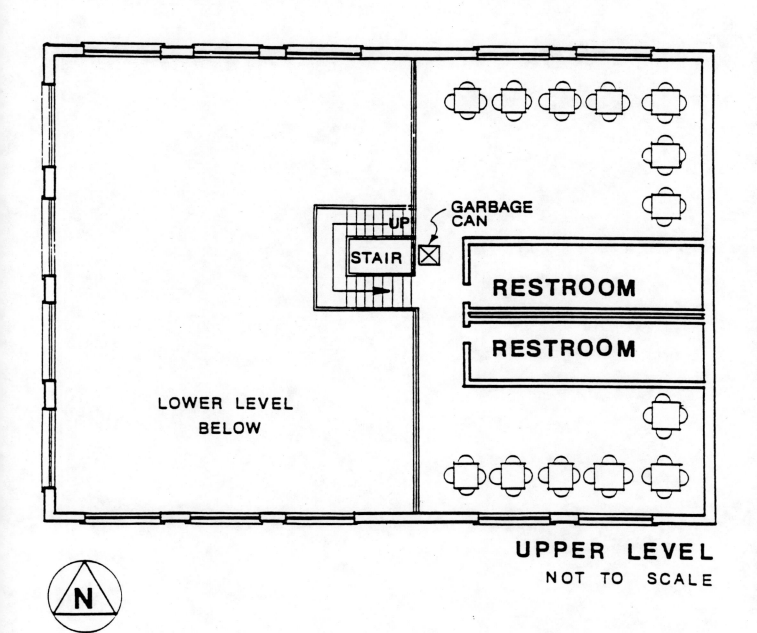

NITA CITY

YR-5
UNIFORM BUILDING CODE

STAIRWAYS

Sec.3306.

(a) **General.** Every stairway having two or more risers serving any building or portion thereof shall conform to the requirements of this section.

EXCEPTION: Stairs or ladders used only to attend equipment are exempt from the requirements of this section.

(b) **Width.** Stairways serving an occupant load of fifty or more shall be not less than forty-four inches in width. Stairways serving an occupant load of forty-nine or less shall be no less than thirty-six inches in width. Private stairways serving an occupant load of less than ten shall be not less than thirty inches in width.

Handrails may project into the required width a distance of 3½ inches from each side of a stairway. Other non-structural projections such as trim and similar decorative features may project into the required width 1½ inches on each side.

(c) **Rise and Run.** The rise of every step in a stairway shall be not less than four inches nor greater than 7½ inches. Except as permitted in Subsections (d) and (f), the run shall be not less than ten inches as measured horizontally between the vertical planes of the furthermost projection of adjacent treads. Except as permitted in Subsections (d), (c), and (f), the largest tread run within any flight of stairs shall not exceed the smallest by more than ⅜ inch. The greatest riser height within any flight of stairs shall not exceed the smallest by more than ⅜ inch.

EXCEPTIONS:

1) Private stairways serving an occupant, load of less than ten and stairways to unoccupied roofs may be constructed with an eight-inch maximum rise and nine-inch minimum run.

2) Where the bottom riser adjoins a sloping public way, walk, or driveway having an established grade and serving as a landing, a variation in height of the bottom and of not more than three inches in every three feet of stairway width is permitted.

(d) Winding Stairways. In Group R, Division 3 Occupancies and in private stairways in Group R, Division 1 Occupancies, winders may be used if the required width of run is provided at a point not more than twelve inches from the end of the stairway where the treads are the narrower, but in no case shall any width of run be less than six inches at any point.

(e) Circular Stairways. Circular stairways may be used as an exit, provided the minimum width of run is not less than ten inches and the smaller radius is not less than twice the width of the stairway. The largest tread width or riser height within any flight of stairs shall not exceed the smallest by more than ⅜ inch.

(f) Spiral Stairways. In Group R, Division 3 Occupancies and in private stairways within individual units of Group R, Division 1 Occupancies, special stairways may be installed. Such stairways may be used for required exits where the area served is limited to four hundred square feet.

The tread must provide a clear walking area measuring at least twenty-six inches from the outer edge of the supporting column to the inner edge of the handrail. A run of at least 7½ inches is to be provided at a point twelve inches from where the tread is narrowest. The rise must be sufficient to provide six-foot, six-inch headroom. The rise shall not exceed 9½ inches.

(g) Landings. Every landing shall have a dimension measured in the direction of travel equal to the width of the stairway. Such dimension need not exceed four feet when the stair has a straight run. A door swinging over a landing shall not reduce the width of the landing to less than one half its required width at any position in its swing nor by more than seven inches when fully open. See Section 3304(h).

EXCEPTION: Stairs serving an unoccupied roof are exempt from these provisions.

(h) Basement Stairways. When a basement stairway and a stairway to an upper story terminate in the same exit enclosure, an approved barrier shall be provided to prevent persons from continuing on into the basement. Directional exit signs shall be provided as specified in Section 3314.

(i) Distance Between Landings. There shall be not more than twelve feet vertically between landings.

(j) **Handrails.** Stairways shall have handrails on each side, and every stairway required to be more than eighty-eight inches in width shall be provided with not less than one intermediate handrail for each eighty-eight inches of required width. Intermediate handrails shall be spaced approximately equally across with the entire width of the stairway.

EXCEPTIONS:

1) Stairways forty-four inches or less in width and stairways serving one individual dwelling unit in Group R, Division 1 or 3 Occupancies may have one handrail, except that such stairways open on one or both sides shall have handrails provided on the open side or sides.

2) Private stairways thirty inches or less in height may have handrails on one side only.

3) Stairways having less than four risers and serving one individual dwelling unit in Group R, Division 1 or 3, or serving Group M Occupancies need not have handrails.

Handrails shall be placed not less than thirty inches nor more than thirty-four inches above the posing of treads. They shall be continuous the full length of the stairs and except for private stairways at least one handrail shall extend not less than six inches beyond the top and bottom risers. Ends shall be returned or shall terminate in newel posts or safety terminals.

The handgrip portion of handrails shall be not less than 1¼ inches nor more than two inches in cross-sectional dimension or the shape shall provide an equivalent gripping surface. The handgrip portion of handrails shall have a smooth surface with no sharp corners.

Handrails projecting from a wall shall have a space of not less than 1½ inches between the wall and the handrail.

CERTIFIED COPY

By *Barbara Carter*
CITY CLERK

DEPOSITION OF JULIE FISHER*

October 21, YR-1

My name is Julie Fisher. My current address is 3415½ Peach Blossom Lane, Macon, Georgia. I was born on March 5, YR-24 in Jackson, Mississippi. I attended school in Jackson, Mississippi, through the end of high school. I graduated from Robert E. Lee High School in Jackson, Mississippi in YR-6. I then attended Emory University in Atlanta, Georgia, graduating in June, YR-2, with a Bachelor of Arts in business. After graduation, I visited a friend in Nita City, Nita. I liked Nita City so much, and was ready for a change from living in the south, that I immediately moved to Nita City and began looking for a job. Beginning September 1, YR-2, I obtained a job as a life insurance application processor at the Fidelity Insurance Company, 321 Front Street, Nita City, Nita. My initial pay was $1,300 per month. This was increased to $1,500 per month beginning December 1, YR-2.

Before I was injured on December 14, YR-2, I had never before suffered an injury of any kind nor had any significant illness other than regular childhood diseases of the measles, mumps, and chicken pox. I had only been to a doctor for regular checkups. The only time I was in a hospital was in YR-6 when I obtained a therapeutic abortion at the Atlanta General Hospital in Atlanta, Georgia.

Right across Front Street from where I worked at the Fidelity Insurance Company, on the corner of Third Avenue and Front Street, there was a fast food hamburger restaurant that was part of the Yankee Doodle Burger chain. I went there for lunch often because I liked the Dandy burger special. It was also inexpensive and quick. That way I could spend the rest of my lunch hour reading. I particularly like Victorian novels. The main disadvantage of the Yankee Doodle Burger Restaurant was that it was always very crowded. I would usually eat there and finish my meal in ten or fifteen minutes and then go to the public library one block away, at Third and Broad Street, to read.

On December 14, YR-2, I went to the Yankee Doodle Burger Restaurant as usual. It was raining lightly that day as it does most of the time during December in Nita City. I got my Dandy burger special and went to sit down. It took me fifteen minutes to get my food that day because the store was jam packed with people, even more than usual. The seating area in the restaurant is built on two levels. Because I do not smoke, I went to sit down in the no-smoking section which is on the upper level. I had

---

*The transcript of Julie Fisher's deposition was excerpted so that only her answers are reprinted here. Assume that this is a true and accurate rendering of those answers.

a hard time finding a place to sit at first. I only was able to find a place to sit by clearing off a table and chair for myself. I ate my lunch quickly that day because I wanted to get out of that crowded place.

I took my tray, paper wrappings, and cup and deposited the garbage in the garbage can that was about three feet from the top of the stairs. I put the tray down on top of a stack of other trays. When I got to the top of the stairs, I started to go down the stairs on the right side. Just as I reached for the handrail, my right foot slipped on something and I fell down the entire length of the stairs on my left side. I reached for the handrail. Before I slipped, I tried to grab onto the handrail to stop myself as I fell down the stairs. My hand just slid down the rail. It felt greasy or oily and was hard to hang on to. I reached over with my left hand to try to grab on with both hands, but they both just slipped off. When I landed at the bottom, a nice old man helped me up. I felt dazed and I sat on the bottom step for a moment to collect my wits. I felt very embarrassed and just went back to work.

Before I got outside the door of the restaurant, I began to wonder why I had fallen. I looked at my right shoe to see if there was anything wrong with my shoe and I saw a greasy smear on the bottom of the shoe. Otherwise, the shoes looked fine. I was wearing flats with about a one-inch heel that had leather soles.

When I got back to work, my left side and the low part of my back started to hurt. I also felt pain in my left wrist. It felt like my wrist was bruised or something. I told my supervisor, Irma Landers, and she recommended I go see a doctor right away. She told me I should go see the doctor she saw for her back problem, whose office was three blocks away; his name is Dr. Brian McBride. I went to see Dr. McBride right away.

Over the next month or so, my left wrist got better and is fine now. My back, however, just kept getting worse. Sometimes it would get a little better and then it would get worse again. I started to get pains in my left leg. I never did go back to work at the Fidelity Insurance Company. I hadn't been working there very long and they told me after about a month that they needed somebody they could count on to come in. I had really liked that job. I enjoyed the kind of work I did and I felt I was some place with a future. They told me they liked my work and my supervisor told me she was going to recommend me for a promotion the next time an appropriate one came up.

One day in March, just before my birthday, I woke up in the middle of the night with real bad back pains and worse pains in my left leg than I had ever had before. I thought maybe the pains would go away by morning, but they didn't. I tried to get hold of Dr. McBride the next morning but found out he was on vacation until the following Monday. I went to the emergency room at the Nita City Memorial Hospital which was just a few blocks from where I lived. They told me to just keep taking the pain pills that Dr. McBride had given me and see him when he got back.

By the end of April I had to get some kind of work in order to pay the rent. Beginning at the first of May, YR-1, I got a job with Ace Collection Agency. My job was as a collection agent. I was only paid $800 per month to begin with, but was told that if I could show that I could do the job, I would get a big raise after two months. I didn't like the job at all; I was trying to get money from people who always said they didn't have money to pay. I knew the kind of position they were in from just having been through several months without work myself. The long hours of sitting and the tensions of the job all seemed to just settle in my back and I couldn't take it. After three weeks, I left the job. Since I had run out of money and it didn't seem like I could keep a job at that time, I moved to live with my sister in Macon, Georgia.

About two weeks after I got back to Georgia, in June of YR-1, in the middle of the night I again started to have real bad back pains. I was numb all over in both legs. I had my sister take me to the Macon General Hospital. They put me in the hospital for about a week and I got a little better. After that, I saw a chiropractor in Macon, Francis Marco, beginning in August of YR-1. I have been seeing him about once a month ever since and his treatment helps some, but not a lot.

The pain in my back is intermittent. I have a pretty much constant sore tenderness most of the time, but occasionally even that goes away. Sometimes it gets real bad and radiates down my left leg. It just comes on when it gets ready to and then it goes away. Before the accident, I liked to stay very active. I enjoyed playing tennis, some jogging, and other sports. One of the reasons I liked living in Nita City is because I like outdoor sports a lot. I like going hiking and camping. I really like dancing. I stayed really socially active because I was a very good dancer. Since my accident, I haven't played tennis at all. Dr. McBride told me I shouldn't. I've done very little physical exercise. Whenever I try to do anything, I end up having to pay for it with excruciating pain for the next several days. I tried dancing only once and ended up flat on my back for four days. I do try to do the exercises that Dr. McBride recommended for my back, but I can't force it to do them too much because it hurts so bad. On the times that I have had sexual intercourse since the accident, it has hurt a lot, which has been frustrating both physically and mentally. My social life has really gone downhill. I have also come under a lot of psychological stress because of my back injury. I'm depressed all of the time because I hurt and because I have financial problems. Also, I feel like I'm not much fun to be around and I don't have as many friends as I used to.

Beginning in October of YR-1, I started to work for Ashley Butler, a retired real estate broker and land developer. He does some work still with his real estate holdings and his real estate agents who have some work for me to do. I do mostly clerical and secretarial work on a part-time basis. I can only handle a few hours a day and he understands. I am paid a salary of $400 per month with the understanding that I will work between fifteen and twenty hours a week. Fortunately, he doesn't keep too close a track because I'm not always able to work that much.

There was no significant person in my life at the time of the accident at Yankee Doodle Burger. I was involved with a guy at Emory but he moved to Los Angeles after graduation. We tried to get up a long distance relationship, but it didn't work. At the end of the summer in YR-2, we called it quits.

I didn't date much after the accident because my injuries made it hard for me to get around. When I moved to Macon, however, I met Jack Ferguson. We hit it off right away and he was very understanding about my injuries. I moved into his apartment in September, YR-1. We have a great relationship. It's really the only good thing in my life. We have talked about getting married and we probably will as soon as his divorce is final. He and his wife have been separated for about three years. They have two little girls: Beth who is eight, and Melanie who is five. The girls live with their mother in Atlanta, but they spend every other weekend with us. I've gotten very close to them.

In July, YR-1, I joined AA in Macon. I had never had a drinking problem until the accident at Yankee Doodle. Then I started drinking a lot because of the pain. Jack and my sister told me they thought it had gotten out of hand. I've been on the wagon since I joined AA, and I've only had two remissions. When my back pain got real bad, I went on a two-day binge in October, YR-1, and a one-day binge in December, YR-1. I think I've got it under control now and I don't expect any more problems.

I never had any back pain before my fall at Yankee Doodle. The only time I was even in a hospital was in the fall of YR-6. That was my freshman year in college. I was involved with a guy and I got pregnant and had an abortion at an abortion clinic. I guess they botched it because I started bleeding real bad the next day and I was hospitalized for a D&C. That turned out fine and I was back to normal in three or four weeks.

I had no other problems in college except when I got caught shoplifting my sophomore year. I tried to steal a Hermes scarf from Saks in Atlanta. They caught me red-handed, so I just confessed. I was placed on the deferred sentencing program, and when I had stayed out of trouble for a year, the whole thing was dropped so I wouldn't have a criminal record.

I wasn't a great student in college but I got by. My grade point at graduation was 2.3. I am sure I would have done better if I had applied myself more, but what with working and going out and socializing, I just wasn't a terrific student.

This deposition was taken in the office of defendant's counsel on January 31, YR-0. This deposition was given under oath, and was read and signed by the deponent.

Certified by:

Anne Dolan

Anne Dolan
Certified Shorthand Reporter
(CSR)

DEPOSITION OF ROGER MITCHELL*

October 25, YR-1

My name is Roger Mitchell. I live at 11352 Elcorn Lane, Lynnwood Manor, Nita City. I am 44 years old. I am currently employed as an area supervisor for the Yankee Doodle Corporation. I was first employed by the Yankee Doodle Corporation in the middle of YR-6. Before that, I had been in the retail business as a shoe salesman and worked in a hardware store after getting out of the Marines in YR-10. I was convicted in YR-9 of federal income tax evasion on my YR-12 income tax. I was fined $2,500 and served three years on probation.

I began with the Yankee Doodle Corporation as a management trainee. I worked as assistant manager at two different Yankee Doodle Burger Restaurants in the Nita area before becoming restaurant manager at the downtown Nita City restaurant at Third and Front Streets. The downtown Nita City Yankee Doodle Burger Restaurant opened in the summer of YR-4, I believe it was August. Before that the location had been a jewelry store.

The downtown Nita City store is unique in several ways. It is the only downtown urban store that I know of that we have in the Nita region. Most of our stores are in suburban shopping malls or along interstate highways. Some of them are also in smaller rural towns. Because of its location, the restaurant serves twice the volume of people in any one day as the other stores. The average for most of our stores is 10,000 people a day. This store serves 22,000 to 24,000 people per day. Finally, this is the only store I know of in the world Yankee Doodle organization that has seating on two floors. As far as I know, the reason for the two-floor arrangement was in order to have more seating area given the cost of floor space in the downtown location. A lot of our customers in the downtown location want to come in and sit down to eat rather than taking out. At other locations, there is a lot more take-out traffic. We tried to conserve space as much as possible and have as much seating area as possible for our customers. Two diagrams, one of the upper level and one of the ground floor, of the store are Exhibits A and B to this deposition.

The Yankee Doodle Corporation is a publicly held corporation that owns and operates a chain of over five hundred fast food restaurants in eighteen states. We are growing at the rate of about fifteen to twenty new stores a year. Our main product line is a variety of burgers and the usual side orders of french fries, onion rings, and soft drink beverages. We also have our

---

*The transcript of Roger Mitchell's deposition was excerpted so that only his answers are reprinted here. Assume that this is a true and accurate rendering of those answers.

own brand of hard pack ice cream that we sell in many varieties. We feel this enables us to compete very favorably with other fast food chains. However, this increases the walk-in traffic significantly and makes crowd management and fast turnaround at the counter a major concern of ours.

Lunch time is the busiest time. The lunch time is from about noon until about two o'clock. Sometimes at lunch the crowds get so massive that it is as much a question of just survival when you are working there as it is trying to serve the people or do a good job. There are just masses and masses of people. My job is to try to keep things flowing. Sometimes I work behind the counter. During lunch time I try to circulate in the seating area to try to make sure that all of the customers are as happy as we can make them. We also have two employees working in the seating area who are constantly cleaning, one in the lower area and one in the upper area. In most stores, there is only one person who cleans, and sometimes only on a part-time basis, in the seating area. The general procedure for the people who do the cleaning is to make a general circuit around the seating area approximately every twenty minutes. They are instructed to and do clean the tables, seats, and spills, if there are any, on the floor. There is no specific instruction with regard to cleaning the stairs or handrail, but it is understood that this is to be done on an as needed basis. Each night the whole restaurant is completely and thoroughly cleaned by the night cleaning crew.

On December 14, YR-2, I was circulating out in the seating area at lunch time. At approximately 12:30 p.m., I noticed a young woman slip or trip at the top right-hand side of the stairs as she was coming down and fall all the way down the stairs. She got right up and walked out of the store. I tried to go up to her to ask her if she was all right, but there were people between us and she got out of there so fast I couldn't stop her. Because she left so quickly, I didn't think much of it at the time.

About three weeks ago, our lawyer told me about this case and that I would have to testify today. As I think back on it, it seems to me that she was in a real hurry as she was coming to the top of the stairs. She didn't seem to be watching where she was going. I don't remember her having her hand on the handrail as she fell and I'm pretty sure I would remember it if she had. Come to think of it, I'm pretty sure I thought at the time that she probably wouldn't have fallen all the way down the stairs if she had her hand on the handrail and stopped herself. I also don't remember anybody helping her up. There wasn't time for that, she was out of there so fast. Also, if I had seen anybody help her up, I would have tried to get his name. We have to be awful careful about people suing us.

In September of YR-1, I was promoted from store manager at that store to area supervisor.

At the request of our lawyer, I did some measurements of the stairs. The stairs are forty-nine inches wide. There are seven stairs going from the first level up to a landing and then seven more stairs going up to the very top. The rise of each stair is 7½ inches and the run is ten inches. This is even throughout the stairs. I saw the young woman fall at the top of the top flight of stairs on her right side as she was coming down. The top of the handrail is thirty inches above the nose of each step. The handrail on the stairs is made out of an oak plank that is 2½ inches wide by 5½ inches deep. It is basically rectangular in cross section with the corners rounded off. The handrail stops right at the top of the top step and right at the bottom of the bottom step where the riser is. That's so people won't bump it when they go walking by. The closest edge of the garbage can to the closest side on the right side of the stairs coming down from the top is forty-two inches. The garbage can is two feet wide and has a cover and a little trap door. The floor material on the stairs is the same as everywhere else in the store. It's a kind of vinyl material. It's never seemed slippery to me.

There has been no change at all in the construction or design of the store since it was opened (and since the accident) with one exception. Right on the inside of the oak plank handrail, we have installed a round metal handrail that is 1¾ inches in diameter. That was done in October of YR-1, after I left as manager.

I am very proud of the safety record we have at Yankee Doodle. As far as I know, nobody has ever been hurt at the downtown Yankee Doodle store or any other store in the region. We try very hard to do everything as safe as possible.

This deposition was taken in the office of plaintiff's counsel on October 25, YR-1. This deposition was given under oath, and was read and signed by the deponent.

Certified by:

Anne Dolan
_____
Anne Dolan
Certified Shorthand Reporter
(CSR)

MERTEC CONSULTING ENGINEERS

1356 COLBY AVENUE • NITA CITY, NITA 99998 • (721) 555-0900

December 7, YR-1

Mr. Donald J. Hamm
Attorney at Law
1600 Columbia Tower
Nita City, Nita 99993

Re: Safety Analysis of Yankee Doodle Restaurant
Client: Julie Fisher

Dear Mr. Hamm:

At your request, I have done a safety analysis of the Yankee Doodle Restaurant at Third and Front Streets in Nita City, Nita. Prior to any investigation, I reviewed the following materials that you provided me:

1. Deposition of Julie Fisher.

2. Deposition of Roger Mitchell, the manager of the restaurant at the time of the accident.

3. Two rough sketches of the layout of the restaurant which are not to scale.

4. Building use permit from the Nita City for the premises.

5. Plans on file with the City Building Department.

On October 30, YR-1 and again on November 25, YR-1, I went to the premises with you with the permission of the restaurant manager and the permission of Sylvia Burton, the lawyer for the restaurant. I measured the stairway to confirm that the measurements made by the restaurant manager and reported in his deposition were correct. These measurements are all the pertinent measurements and they are correct. I performed coefficient of friction tests on the top stair at the point where you advised me that Ms. Fisher had slipped. This point was confirmed by information from Ms. Fisher's deposition.

On the second occasion, I re-examined the stairway after the additional handrail was installed. I also observed general operations of the restaurant. I spent approximately one hour on each visit.

My conclusions are as follows:

1.   Floor Material. The coefficient of friction tests that I performed were to determine the slipperiness of the flooring material on the stairway. This is the same flooring material that is used throughout the restaurant. I tested the flooring material using Ms. Fisher's shoe that she was wearing at the time. I did the tests (1) on dry floor, (2) after the floor had been wetted with a volume of water of approximately ¼ cup, and (3) with several drops of common cooking oil of the type that is usually used for deep-fat frying in fast food restaurants. The tests revealed that when the floor was dry, it provided a reasonably safe and non-slippery walking surface. However, when there was either water or cooking oil on the floor, it was approximately as slippery as if the same shoe were on glare ice.

2.   Handrail. The handrail in existence at the time of Ms. Fisher's fall consisted of an oak plank that was nominally three inches by six inches. After finishing, the plank measured 2½ by 5½ inches. It was covered with a polyurethane finish. The handrail was secured to the starts by uprights at the top stair, the bottom stair, and one middle stair. Between the uprights there was a shield of thick plate glass which extended the whole distance between the uprights.

The maintenance of the handrail and the cross-sectional shape of the handrail do not meet the requirements of the most recent edition of the Uniform Building Code. The requirements code for stairs in general is set forth in Chapter 33. The handgrip portion of the handrails are required to be not less than 1¼ inches nor more than two inches in cross-sectional dimension and are required to be round or oval in shape. Additionally, at least one handrail is required to extend at least six inches beyond the top and the bottom riser of the stairway. These code requirements are safety requirements and are very important to the safety of the person walking up and down stairs.

The cross-sectional shape and dimension requirements are important to provide a handrail that can be readily grasped by a person walking up and down the stairs. The handrail should be round or oval so that the person's hand can completely surround it for a secure grip. Its size should not be more than two inches so that it's not too large to grasp securely and safely.

The extension of the handrail is very important. Studies, particularly an authoritative study by the National Bureau of Standards in YR-6 on stair safety, have shown that most stairway accidents occur at the top of the stairway. This is the most dangerous and critical point for a person walking down the stairway. It is important that the person be able to grasp the handrail before the first stair down the stairway so that the person can steady himself or herself before the first stair.

Because the subject handrail does not extend beyond the top riser, that was not possible in this case. In my opinion, the condition of the handrail (including the violations of the Building Code) constituted a very dangerous condition which subjected people walking up and down the stairs to a danger of injury from falling.

The newly-installed round handrail meets the Building Code requirements. It is a reasonable addition and significantly improves the safety of the stairway.

3. Stairs. I confirmed that the measurements of the stairs by the restaurant manager as reported in his deposition were correct. The measurement of the stairs meets the minimum requirements of the Safety Code. The stairs are as steep as permitted by the Code. Although the stairs do not themselves necessarily create a safety risk, they are of a condition which should be considered when analyzing safety with the entire structure in mind.

Here, it appeared to me that the design of the stairs was to use the least amount of area in order to provide the most seating possible. Accordingly, the stairs were steep. The Yankee Doodle organization did a very good job in designing the entire store, including the stairs, to be attractive. I am sure it is a profitable operation, given the crowds of people that I saw. However, more attention should have been given to safety on the stairs because of their steepness.

Because of the steepness of the stairs, the slipperiness of the floor when contaminated, and the risk of spilling, see Items 4 and 5, I would recommend that for the safety of the customers, non-skid strips be applied to the nosing of the stairs. These non-skid strips can be purchased for $1 a piece at most building supply stores in the city. They are easily applied and help greatly in reducing slips and falling accidents.

4.   Refuse Container. There is a refuse container forty-two inches from the area at the top of the steps. Because the Yankee Doodle customers are expected to bus their own tables, they must use this refuse container to throw away their refuse. This creates a high likelihood of spillage of foreign substances in the area that will probably be tracked to the top of the stairs. When I examined the area in front of the refuse container at the top of the stairs, on both occasions I saw several spots which appeared to be grease, animal fat, or cooking oil that varied between ½ inch and two inches in diameter. On one occasion, I saw a spill of either water or soft drink or melted ice from a soft drink that was approximately ½ cup next to the refuse container. Someone had stepped in the spill and tracked it to the top of the stairs. This sort of spillage can be reasonably anticipated to exist at the top of the stairs given the nature of the restaurant and the location of the refuse container.

I would recommend that, for the safety of the customers, the refuse container be moved to a location at least ten to fifteen feet from the top of the stairs and that a safety mat or carpet be placed in front of it to catch any spills. This would significantly reduce tracking of spills to the top of the stairs.

5.   Operations. On the two occasions I was in the restaurant, I watched the clean-up person both upstairs and downstairs. There were two clean-up people. The person did an excellent job of cleaning the top of the tables and the chairs. However, on no occasion did I see the clean-up person pay any attention to cleaning the floor.

Because there was one person upstairs and one person downstairs, the clean-up people did not travel up and down the stairs. On the occasions I was in the restaurant, the handrail felt greasy to my touch. I did not see the clean-up person wipe the handrail at any time. It would be my recommendation that, for the safety of the customers, the clean-up people be instructed to pay regular attention to cleaning floors, particularly at critical areas such as at the top of the stairs and in front of the refuse container. Additionally, the handrail should be wiped at least once every half hour. It can be anticipated that the handrail will become greasy. The type of product sold at Yankee Doodle Burgers is finger-food. It is generally greasy. For this reason, the customers' hands tend to become greasy and the grease is transferred to the handrail as they use the stairs.

In summary, I concluded that the combination of the steepness of the stairs, the slipperiness of the floor with foreign material on it, and the location of the refuse container made the entire construction of the stairway, given the operation of the restaurant, an unreasonably dangerous condition. The danger could have been obviated by the simple and inexpensive expedients of:

1.   Applying non-slip strips to the nosing of the stairs.

2.   Moving the refuse container away from near the top of the stairs.

3.   Putting a safety mat or carpet in front of the refuse container.

4.   Instructing the clean-up personnel to clean the floor in critical areas and wipe the handrail.

Wholly separate from these conditions, the condition of the handrail is a violation of the Building Code and constituted an unreasonably dangerous condition which was a severe risk to the safety of the customers. The failure to have the handrail extend beyond the top of the top step and the unwieldy shape of the handrail, both in violation of the Building Code, made the handrail unsafe. The changes in the handrail after the accident improved the situation to eliminate many of the safety risks.

The combination of the general design of the stairs with the operation of the restaurant and the unsafe condition of the handrail made the area at the top of the stairs of the Yankee Doodle Restaurant very unsafe. It was an accident waiting to happen.

Yours very truly,

Merlin J. Lombard

Merlin J. Lombard, C.P.E.

MJL/mfd

ADDITIONAL BACKGROUND INFORMATION AND QUALIFICATIONS
OF MERLIN J. LOMBARD, C.P.E.

I completed a five-year course of study at Stanford University, receiving a Bachelor of Arts in architecture and Bachelor of Science in civil engineering in YR-33. I then went to work for Harland Emerson & Associates, an architectural and structural engineering firm in San Francisco. I specialized in the structural and architectural design of industrial plants and factories.

In YR-28, I was hired by the Amalgamated Electric Corporation as a design engineer to oversee the design and construction of their production facilities throughout the United States. I stayed in that position, eventually becoming Vice President for Production Design in YR-22 and remained in that position until YR-16. In YR-16, I was asked by the Chairman of the Board to be project manager to set up three new production facilities in Iran for the corporation. There, I was the first project manager and ultimately general manager of the Iran Electronic Corporation, a wholly-owned subsidiary of the Amalgamated Electric Corporation.

During my entire period with the Amalgamated Electric Corporation, I acted as a member of and chaired various safety committees for the corporation and worked on joint employer/union safety committees for the employer. I insisted on a sophisticated safety program for the Iran Electronic Corporation. When designing factories, I took special care to consider safety. I am familiar with all types of building and construction codes.

With the advent of political unrest in Iran, I retired from the Amalgamated Electric Corporation in YR-8. I returned to Nita City, Nita, where I had been born, and founded Mertec Engineering, an engineering consulting firm which employs twenty-five engineers and consults on all manners of engineering. Approximately 25% of the work performed by the firm is forensic work, including accident reconstruction and any factors in safety analysis for the legal and insurance industries. Forensic work is an area of our business that shows tremendous growth potential.

I am a certified professional engineer in civil and structural engineering in the states of California and Nita. I have a special expertise in safety design.

I charge $100 per hour for every hour I work. I will have spent fifteen hours in review and analysis of this case prior to trial. I have testified on many occasions for both plaintiff and defendant.

I do not know Thomas Newburg or his reputation.

BOTTOMS, NEWBURG & ASSOCIATES

Architects
4333 Javens Street
Nita City, Nita 99990
(721) 555-0001

December 20, YR-1

Ms. Sylvia Butler
Attorney at Law
Suite 500, Buck Tower
Nita City, Nita 99993

Re: *Yankee Doodle Restaurant Renovation*
        Lawsuit by Julie Fisher

Dear Ms. Butler:

This letter is written to you as a summary of my conclusions as expressed to you in our meeting of November 20, YR-1. Since our meeting, I have reviewed the report of Merlin Lombard, C.P.E., and have again reviewed the plans and specifications for the restaurant conversion project. I also again visited the restaurant and have researched the Uniform Building Code. You previously provided me with the depositions of Ms. Fisher and Roger Mitchell. I am well familiar with all the documentation concerning the design for the conversion to the current Yankee Doodle Restaurant at Third and Front Streets in Nita City.

As you know, I was the consulting architect who had the major responsibility for the design work on the Yankee Doodle Restaurant conversion. I have previously designed three individual Yankee Doodle Restaurants and have been a consultant for a general operational design for the new Yankee Doodle Restaurants to be constructed in the future. I am very familiar with design features in restaurants, hotels, and motels in this area. This experience and knowledge was utilized during design of the Yankee Doodle Restaurant conversion from the former jewelry store location.

Prior to construction of the restaurant, the plans and specifications were submitted to the City of Nita for review. All of the appropriate licenses and permits were received. The plans were reviewed by the City and approved by the Superintendent of Buildings who issued a building use permit, a certified copy of which is attached. It was my understanding and belief that the plans for the Yankee Doodle Restaurant conversion complied with all applicable codes, laws, and regulations at the time of construction. The construction was in complete conformance with the plan; there was no variation. I inspected the construction at various times to confirm this.

The handrail on the stairs is a common handrail design for restaurants and hotels. It is very attractive and functional. I know three department stores in Nita City, four restaurants, and two hotels in other parts of the state of Nita that have exactly the same handrail design. I have never heard a report of anyone ever having any trouble using these handrails or claiming to be injured because of the design of the handrail. This handrail design has been common in the hotel and restaurant industry since at least YR-10. In my opinion, the handrail design is safe and provides a safe means of steadying one's self as one walks down the stairs. No handrail can guarantee that a person who falls as a result of inattention or hurry will be stopped before falling all the way down the stairs.

It is true that the handrail is in technical violation of the Building Code. However, this violation is not significant or substantial. Nonetheless, after consultation with the northwest regional manager for Yankee Doodle Corporation, Jerome Peters, I advised the addition of a new handrail at the downtown Nita City Yankee Doodle Restaurant in order to avoid any possibility of an ordinance violation citation by the Nita City building officials. Such a citation would carry a civil penalty that would be greater than the installation cost of the new handrail. Despite my advice to install the new handrail, it is my opinion that the originally-designed handrail was safe.

Close attention was paid to the Building Code concerning construction of the stairs. The stairs are in complete compliance with the Building Code with regard to the steepness of the stairs. The design decision concerning the dimensions of the rise and run of the stairs was made with the consideration of the Building Code and the operational requirements of the restaurant. The cost of the space in downtown Nita City and the need for as much seating area as possible made it desirable to not occupy a large area with a stairway. Accordingly, the stairway was designed to be safe and in compliance with the Building Code, but to take as little space as possible.

The flooring material on the floor and the stairs is a slip-resistant material. I have used it in many other restaurant construction projects and it provides a safe walking surface. Specifications provided by the manufacturer indicate that the coefficient of friction tests conducted on the material confirm that it provides a safe walking surface.

With regard to other specific criticisms set forth in Mr. Lombard's report, it is my opinion that the location of the refuse container is safe. It was designed to be located in that area in order to accommodate the convenience of the customers in busing their own tables and to promote the efficient operation of the restaurant with regard to traffic flow. It provides a safe and convenient way for the customers to deposit their refuse. The opening in the container is large enough to minimize any spillage while the customers deposit their refuse. In all the times I have been in the restaurant, I have never seen a customer spill anything. A carpet or mat in front of the refuse container would be unsightly and unnecessary. In addition, it would in itself cause a tripping hazard because such carpets tend to get bunched up and may well trip a customer. The same is true for the so-called safety strips or non-skid strips for the nosing of the stairs. They are unsightly and constitute a tripping hazard. They can stop a person's foot too quickly and trip them as they walk down the stairs. In my opinion, such strips provide too much friction for a safe walking surface. Furthermore, the strips tend to become loose with time, causing additional tripping hazards. Where they are used, I usually advise the customer that they must be replaced every six weeks to two months, but that such trouble and expense is unnecessary.

In conclusion, it is my opinion that the design and construction of the stairs at the time of Ms. Fisher's fall was safe and reasonable. The design and construction of the stairs was a usual, common, design in the hotel and restaurant industry.

Sincerely,

Thomas Newburg

TSN:ppb

BACKGROUND INFORMATION AND QUALIFICATIONS
OF THOMAS NEWBURG

I graduated from the University of Nita with a bachelor's degree in architecture in YR-29. I then served four years in the Army and was discharged with the rank of Captain in the Army Corps of Engineers. During my time in the Army, I assisted in the design and construction of several facilities used for the housing of troops and many marshals. In YR-25, I returned to school and received a master's degree in architecture from the University of California at Berkeley. In YR-23, I went to work for an architectural firm in Seattle, Washington, and worked there for four years. I then moved to Nita City and founded my own architecture firm with Jeremy Bottoms, my partner. The firm employs six architects besides my partner and me. The firm specializes in design of restaurants, hotels, and motels. I am special consultant to three fast food restaurant chains and operational design of chain stores. I provide a special consulting service to franchisees of one of the restaurant chains. I delivered a paper to the American Architectural Association annual meeting in YR-6 entitled, "Aesthetic Design of Fast Food Restaurants."

I am not charging for my time spent analyzing and testifying in this case. I am doing it as a service to a valued client, Yankee Doodle Corporation.

I do not know Merlin Lombard personally, but I am familiar with the reputation of Mertec Engineering, which is excellent in the consulting engineering field.

I have testified in court before on three occasions concerning cost overruns in construction projects. I have never testified in a personal injury case.

BRIAN McBRIDE, M.D.

Orthopedic Surgeon
Plaza Medical Tower
Nita City, Nita 99992
(721) 555-2028

December 9, YR-1

Mr. Donald J. Hamm
Attorney at Law
1600 Columbia Tower
Nita City, Nita 99993

Re: Julie Fisher

Dear Mr. Hamm:

This is in response to your request for a complete and detailed report concerning Ms. Fisher.

I first saw Ms. Fisher on December 14, YR-2, on referral from another patient. She complained of pain in her left lower back and also some pain in her left wrist. Her symptoms began just after noon that day when she fell down some stairs at the nearby Yankee Doodle Burger. She stated that she slipped at the top of the stairs as she was reaching for the handrail. She managed to grab onto the railing as she was falling, but could not hang on to her grip. She fell all the way to the bottom of the stairs, a distance of eight to ten feet.

She rested for a moment on the step and then said she was embarrassed by the crowd, and left to go back to work. When she got back at work, her back began to hurt so much that she came in to see me. Fortunately, I had a cancellation and was able to see her.

Her medical history was essentially negative. She simply had regular check-ups and gynecological exams.

Examination

The patient is 5 foot, 5 inches tall and weighs 120 pounds. There is evidence of spasm in her back muscles on the left. She is tender in this area. Her motion in the back is markedly limited, particularly on flexion and lateral bending to the left. Reflexes are normal.

There is slight swelling in her wrist. She has some tenderness in the area. X-rays of the left wrist, forearm, and elbow are negative for evidence of fracture. Films of the lumbar spine are essentially negative.

She was advised that she had a contusion of her flank and wrist. The wrist was wrapped with an Ace bandage. She was advised about back exercises and told to take aspirin for pain. She was to return in one week.

What follows is a summary of my office notes for the next several months:

12/21/YR-2: Patient states she is a little better. Her back isn't quite as sore, but she has some radiation into her left leg. Her wrist bothers her much less. She is to continue to exercise her back. As soon as she feels able, she may return to work.

1/13/YR-1: She is complaining of considerable pain in her back, mainly over the left posterior superior spine. She states her wrist is doing pretty well. There is definite localized pain in the left posterior superior spine. There is evidence of muscle spasm. This area was injected with an anesthetic and muscle relaxant. She is to stay off work two months.

2/28/YR-1: Patient seen with a complaint over the Achilles tendon and in the gastric muscles on the left. This began last evening while getting dinner. She did not twist or bend or injure herself, she just began to ache. She wrapped the Ace bandage that I had given her for her wrist on her leg, but it's still sore today. Pending examination, there is no swelling. There is tenderness over the Achilles tendon and tenderness in the gastric muscles. Plantar flexion causes increased discomfort. This may represent an Achilles tendinitis or possible phlebitis or be referred pain from the back injury which would indicate a disc problem. She was put on Butazolidin alka, 1 t.i.d. Leg rewrapped with Ace bandage. Return if no improvement.

3/7/YR-1: States she isn't having as much pain down the calf of her left leg but now has pain into the left iliolumbar area. She has some radiation down her leg. Last week she went to the Nita City Memorial Emergency Room and was given further instructions on back exercises and told to return to see me. She was also given 12 Percodan at the ER. She is very tender in the left iliolumbar area and reflexes are present and equal. I again injected the area. I advised her of the addictive nature of Percodan and suggested that she use it sparingly. I did not continue the prescription. Stay off work and return in one week.

3/10/YR-1: States she is a little better since the injection. She still is getting pain in her back and down her leg. She is to continue with flexion stretching. She should avoid laying on her abdomen. She states she is most comfortable lying on her side with the left leg drawn up. She was given a five-day supply day of norgestic forte, 1 q.i.d.

3/24/YR-1: Got along pretty well until two days ago when she began to experience pain in her left leg again, with radiation down the left leg to the back of the knee. She is still tender in the left iliolumbar area. This sight was again injected with carbocaine and aristocort. There is some numbness on her left foot. Stay off work.

4/11/YR-1: The patient has been feeling much better since her injection on her last visit. She still has generalized aching in her left lumbar area. She has been off work since her accident and I feel this is reasonable. She indicates that her financial situation makes it difficult for her to stay off work. I feel that she can try to return to some type of light duty on a trial basis at the end of this month.

5/18/YR-1: Patient has gotten a job where she sits and talks on the phone all day and does some typing. She said it's very emotionally trying. On examination, she is very tender in her left iliolumbar area again. She reports radiation pain down the left leg. Straight leg raising is negative on the right but positive on the left in both the supine and sitting positions at 50˚. I again injected her.

I advised the patient that she probably tried to return to work too soon and that a job where she has to sit all day may not be the best for her. She should stay off work at least another two months and return to see me then or on an as needed basis. Ideally, if she returns to work she should have a job where she could move around.

I did not see the patient again until she returned to see me on examination on November 30, YR-1, at your request. The patient advised me that after leaving her job in May, she returned to Georgia to live with her sister. She had a one-week hospitalization in June of last year and has been seeing a chiropractor on a monthly basis since then. She said that her lower back hurts most of the time with occasional radiation into her left leg. She said chiropractic manipulations help some, but sometimes do bring on the radiation for a period of time. She states the airplane ride from Georgia yesterday brought on sharp pains in her left low back and radiation of the pain into her left leg.

On examination, I found that straight leg raising was positive on the left in both supine and sitting positions at 50˚ but negative on the right. She had admitted diminution of sensation over the lateral border of her left foot. Both findings correspond to nerve root irritation at the first sacral nerve root and probably a disc injury. This is a definite abnormal finding.

Given the continued problems and findings concerning low back injury, I felt further tests ought to be done to determine whether there is a disc injury where disc surgery would be appropriate. I referred her to Nita City Memorial for a CT scan. The results showed some bulging at the L5-S1 level, confirming the neurological finding of irritation of the first sacral nerve root. I have reviewed the films personally and find them to be of Dr. Noel's usual high quality. Only when given the high quality of film can the small, but distinct, disc bulging be determined.

Conclusion

Ms. Fisher is a very pleasant young woman who I have been pleased to be able to treat. Her attitude throughout has been one of being very motivated to recover. I have no doubt about the sincerity and honesty of her report of her symptoms.

In my opinion, Ms. Fisher suffered from a significant trauma and strain of her left lumbar spine as a direct result of her fall on December 14, YR-2. This strain has progressed to a herniating-type disc injury. In my opinion, Ms. Fisher has an injury to her disc which has caused a weakening in the disc such that it periodically bulges and irritates the first sacral nerve root. In my opinion, the CT scan has confirmed this.

The prognosis for a full recovery is not good. Hopefully, Mother Nature will help out and the weak area of her disc will strengthen such that the disc no longer bulges. However, in my opinion, it is more probable than not her symptoms will remain the same or worsen in the future. This will restrict the amount and type of activities she can do.

I have recommended she purchase a back brace and wear it at all times. I also feel she should continue to do back exercises as she has done and increase the amount of exercise as it is tolerated. She is not at this time a surgical candidate, however. In my opinion, there is a 30-40% chance that, were she to continue to be my patient, I would recommend surgery in the future. Were surgery performed, it would cost $4,000-$5,000 and require a two-week hospital stay and three months of convalescence.

Very truly yours,

Brian McBride, M.D.

Brian McBride, M.D.

BRIAN McBRIDE, M.D.
BACKGROUND INFORMATION

I graduated from the University of Oregon in YR-42. I then went to medical school at the University of Nita and graduated in YR-37. I did my internship and residency at Harborview Hospital in San Francisco in orthopedic surgery which I completed in YR-33. I then entered the Army as a Major and was stationed at Fort Bragg, where I was Assistant Chief of Orthopedics for two years. In YR-30, I moved to Nita City and entered private practice as an orthopedic surgeon. I am licensed as a physician and surgeon in the State of Nita, and am a member of the American Board of Orthopedic Surgery and the American Academy of Orthopedic Surgery and several other orthopedic societies. I am Board-certified in orthopedic surgery. I have been in private practice ever since YR-30.

I do not testify on a regular basis. I have testified over the years approximately ten to fifteen times for my patients. I have done an approximately equal amount of defense medical examinations. I will not do the medical legal consultation for a plaintiff in a personal injury case. I do not like being involved in litigation and avoid it at all cost. The three times I have done defense medical examinations have been for the firm in which Sylvia Burton is a partner.

I am familiar with Rita Moran and have little respect for her because, in my opinion, she is not a doctor but a professional witness whose opinion depends on who hires her. I do charge for my time while testifying at the rate of $100 per hour.

RITA C. MORAN, M.D., F.A.C.S.
Diplomate American Board of Orthopedic Surgery
3801 Cantell Avenue, Suite 321
Nita City, Nita 99996
(721) 555-7702

April 28, YR-1

Ms. Sylvia Burton
Attorney at Law
Suite 500, Buck Tower
Nita City, Nita 99993

Re: Julie Fisher
Date of Exam: April 28, YR-1

Dear Ms. Burton:

At your request, I examined the above-referenced 23-year-old
female on the above-mentioned date. The patient states she
was injured five months ago when she slipped or tripped at
the top of a flight of stairs in a fast-food restaurant in
downtown Nita City and fell all the way down the stairs. She
is very emphatic that she tried to grab onto the handrail as
she fell down the stairs, but her hand slipped off. She
repeated four times and insisted I write down in my notes
that she tried to grab onto the handrail. She reminded me
again at the end of the examination to write down that she
tried to grab onto the handrail.

She experienced no immediate pain or discomfort and returned
to work. After she returned to work, on the advice and
recommendation of her supervisor, she went to see Brian
McBride, M.D.

I have reviewed Dr. McBride's office notes from his
treatment to date and have seen the Emergency Room report
for the visit to the Emergency Room of the Nita City
Memorial Hospital in early March of this year.

Past History and Social History

Patient is a college graduate from Georgia. She aborted a
pregnancy in YR-6 but otherwise has a negative medical
history. She has only worked for four months before her
present injury and has not worked since. She states she does
not smoke and denies more than social drinking or use of
controlled substances.

Complaints

The patient states that by the time she got to Dr. McBride's office on the day of her fall, her left wrist hurt and she had pain in her lower back. She states the pain in her lower back got continually worse over the next several months and occasionally radiated into her left leg. She describes occasions when the pain was so severe that she could not walk and she felt numb all over her body, particularly in both lower extremities. She states the pain and numbness in her legs only occurs occasionally and that the pain in her back comes and goes. Sometimes it is a sharp pain and sometimes it is a dull ache. It seems to come and go by itself, without being brought on by any particular activity.

Her present chief complaint at the time of the examination is a mild, dull ache in her lower back. She states strenuous activity, particularly dancing, aggravates the pain and makes it sharp. It is not aggravated by coughing. She states she has pain in her buttocks area if she sits for extended periods or drives a car.

Radiographs

Adequate Roentgengrams have been taken by Dr. McBride and at the Nita City Memorial Hospital. These were available for review. They were entirely negative and showed normal lumbar spine.

Physical Examination

The patient is a 23-year-old female of average height and weight. At the time of the examination, she was in no acute distress. She walks well without a limp and rises well on her toes, maintaining balance. She has good coordination. She can squat and rise from a kneeling position. Knee jerks and ankle jerks are active and equal. Thigh and calf measurements are equal at the same level. There is good quadriceps strength against resistance. There is no evidence of edema. Knee jerks and ankle jerks are quite active and equal on both sides. Movement at the hip joints is free and easy on both sides. No particular pain is referred in the back by hyperflexion of the thighs on the abdomen. In the prone position, straight leg raising does not cause unusual pain referable to the back area.

Straight leg raising in the sitting position is negative on the right. Patient complains of some pain with straight leg raising in the sitting position on the left at 60˚. There is no unusual tenderness to palpation. The patient points out a spot at the base of the buttocks on the left side as being the area that bothers her with a general dull ache. She has received conservative treatment from Dr. McBride which appears to be reasonable. She is advised to continue the present management.

The neurological examination is essentially negative except that the patient reports an area of minimal diminished sensation on her left foot. This cannot be reproduced with certainty when the patient is asked to close her eyes.

Diagnosis

1. Mild lower back strain, probably related to fall of December YR-2, essentially resolved.

2. Lack of objective findings of changes in gait, limping, function, x-ray findings, reproducible neurological findings, or range of motion restriction.

3. Probably functional overlay to minimal physical injury. Many of the complaints reported by the patient which were not present at the day of the examination have hysterical qualities. Possibly secondary gain.

Comment

Most of this young woman's symptoms are subjective and not accompanied by objective findings. The positive straight leg raising on the left in the sitting position is not reproducible in the prone position and, therefore, suspect. The same is true for the positive finding of the diminution of sensation on the left foot.

A psychological evaluation may be warranted. This young woman's complaints have hysterical qualities and appear to have a psychological rather than an organic basis. It is my opinion that many of her subjective complaints will subside after the conclusion of her lawsuit.

In my opinion, she has made an excellent recovery from her minor injuries from the fall and has no residual disability and will require no further medical treatment. In my opinion, she was able to work at her regular job after no more than one month off work and probably after one week.

Sincerely,

Rita Moran, M.D.

Rita Moran, M.D.

RM/slj

RITA C. MORAN, M.D., F.A.C.S.
Diplomate American Board of Orthopedic Surgery
3801 Cantell Avenue, Suite 321
Nita City, Nita 99996
(721) 555-7002

December 7, YR-1

Ms. Sylvia Burton
Attorney at Law
Suite 500, Buck Tower
Nita City, Nita 99993

Re: Julie Fisher
     Supplemental Report

Dear Ms. Burton:

I have reviewed the original films of the CT scan of Ms.
Fisher performed by Dr. Simon on December 3, YR-1, and have
also reviewed Dr. Noel's report. In my opinion, the CT scan
is totally normal. With all due reference to Dr. Noel, for
whom I have the highest respect, in my opinion the CT scan
shows no bulging. What appears to be a possible bulging of
the L5-S1 level is due to the poor quality of the films.

Sincerely,

Rita Moran, M.D.

Rita Moran, M.D.

RM/slj

BACKGROUND INFORMATION AND QUALIFICATIONS OF RITA MORAN, M.D.

I graduated from medical school at the University of Edinborough, Scotland, in YR-25. I did an internship at the Women's Hospital of London, London, England. In YR-24 to YR-19, I was Chief Orthopedic Resident. I then moved to Nita City, Nita, where I opened a private practice in orthopedics. I am a Board-certified orthopedic surgeon and was Board-certified in YR-15. I was continuously in the practice of orthopedic surgery until YR-5 when I retired from the active practice of medicine and now only do evaluations and consultation by referral. I no longer perform surgery. I receive referrals from other orthopedic surgeons to evaluate on-going patients. I also do examinations from the Department of Labor and Industries Industrial Insurance claimants. I perform medical examinations for testimony in personal injury lawsuits. I have testified numerous times for both the plaintiff and the defendant. I receive $350 per hour for each hour I spend out of court.

As far as I know, Dr. McBride is a competent physician. I think he lost a medical malpractice case for performing unnecessary surgery once, however.

NITA CITY HOSPITAL

N

Ninth Avenue at Cherry Street
Nita City, Nita 99996
(721) 555-4121

Exhibit 1

EMERGENCY ROOM RECORD

PATIENT:	Fisher, Julie	DATE:	3-2-YR-1
	3690 Demsey Street	TIME:	8:00 am
	Nita City, Nita	ER NO.:	3426-82
DOB:	3-5-YR-24	EMPLOYER:	None
SS NO.:	496-32-5281		
PERSONAL		DISPOSITION:	Home
PHYSICIAN:	McBride	DIAGNOSIS:	LBP

HISTORY:

This woman's chief complaint is of lower back pain. The patient gives a history of falling down some stairs some time in December. She has been seeing an orthopedic surgeon in Nita City off and on since that time. A few days ago the patient began complaining of pain in the lower portion of her left leg. She was seen by her physician in Nita City and evaluated. The possibility of phlebitis in the lower portion of the leg was considered. The patient was started on Butazolidin alka therapy. Last night the patient developed rather severe pain down the entire posterolateral aspect of the left leg and pain in the low back. She attempted to reach her physician this morning but wasn't able to do so and then was brought in by ambulance to this hospital. On arrival here, the patient exhibited a great deal of pain behavior. Examination of the back was difficult because the patient did react rather prominently to any kind of a maneuver or palpation. There did appear to be rather significant lumbar spasm. Examination of the leg found there was no evidence of swelling, redness, or heat. The patient complained of tenderness but was not consistent in the localization of the tenderness. Homan's sign was not definitely not positive. There is no edema of her foot or of her leg. Straight leg raising of the legs is difficult to evaluate. Lumbar spine films were taken which appear normal to this examiner.

IMPRESSION:

Back pain, pain in the left leg, etiology undetermined. The patient was advised that there is a possibility of disc injury; however, there is no evidence of serious pressure on nerve roots at this time. She was advised to go home, go back to bed rest, continue the Butazolidin alka. She was advised of other symptomatic measures and will see her physician in the next three to four days.

C. Thorstenson, M.D.
ER Physician

NITA CITY HOSPITAL

Ninth Avenue at Cherry Street
Nita City, Nita 99996
(721) 555-4121

Exhibit 2

DEPARTMENT OF RADIOLOGY

REPORT

Fisher, Julie M33
12-3-YR-1

X-RAY # 42988-YR-1
OP # 807892-6
DR. McBRIDE

PRELIMINARY LUMBOSACRAL SPINE: 3 films.

Preliminary films of the lumbosacral spine show five true nonrib bearing lumbar vertebrae. The disc spaces are well preserved and the lumbar vertebral bodies appear normal.

IMPRESSION: normal lumbosacral spine.

CT OF THE LUMBAR SPINE WITHOUT CONTRACT: Multiple scans.

Particular attention is directed to the lower three lumbar interspaces. No abnormality seen at the L3-4 interspace or at the L4-5 interspace. Possible minimal disc bulging at the L5-S1 level. At the lumbosacral junction no disc herniation is demonstrated.

IMPRESSION:

Very minimal disc bulging L5-S1 level without true evidence of disc herniation, compression of thecal sac or displacement of nerve roots.

Simon Noel, M.D.

Simon Noel, M.D.
Chief of Radiology
12-3-YR-1 cas

Exhibit 3

MACON GENERAL HOSPITAL
MACON, GEORGIA

HISTORY AND PHYSICAL

PATIENT: Fisher, Julie   HOSPITAL #:   483-6290

PHYSICIAN: Crane   ADMITTED: 6-10-YR-1

ADMITTING DIAGNOSIS: Low back strain.

HISTORY:

This patient, a 23 year-old female, has a history of low back discomfort. I believe that she was mainly functional when I last saw her. She apparently received some treatment in Nita City, Nita. When it was felt it was time for her to return to work she left Nita City. She apparently came in on 6-3-YR-1 with low back pain and was treated as an emergency room patient. She was referred to my office and she, indeed, had an appointment to see me on 6-12-YR-1. However, last night she began to have increased pain and came in by ambulance. She told the emergency room physician she was numb all over her lower extremities bilaterally and she could not move at all and she screamed on touching her. She also had some numbness of the left upper extremity and obvious other hysterical complaints. It was necessary to admit her to the hospital on the basis of these complaints.

Today she seems to be alert and quite oriented. She states she has no allergies. She takes no medications other than some pain medications which I had given her. She has never had any operations. She denies any history of rheumatic fever, tuberculosis, or other serious disease. She denies a history of passing out, head, eyes, ears, nose, or throat problems. She also denies any history of heart disease. She states she has had bronchitis in the past, but otherwise has no other lung disease.

Gastrointestinal system was normal. The genito-urinary system reveals the patient has had a diagnosis of endometriosis in the past.

PHYSICAL EXAMINATION:

General:
She is a well-developed, well-nourished female. She prefers not to get up to walk due to discomfort in the low back.

HEENT:
The pupils are equal and react to light.

Vital Signs:
Blood pressure, 160/86. Respiratory rate, 22 per minute. Pulse, 100 per minute.

Temperature:
97.80 on admission.

She lifts her head from the pillow without pain.

Chest:
Clear to auscultation.

Heart:
There is no cardiomegaly. There are no heart murmurs.

Abdomen:
Soft and non-tender. There is no organomegaly.

Neurological:
Straight leg raising on the right is 15°, the left is 10°. The patient has hypesthesia, probably most marked in the S1 distribution on the left. She has good muscle strength of the extensor hallucis longus to the os anterior peroneal and quadriceps muscle groups, however, she screams with pain on dorsiflexion of the left ankle in the supine position.

She has 1+ knee jerks bilaterally and 0 ankle jerks bilaterally.

IMPRESSION:
Low back strain.

PLAN:
This patient has many hysterical qualities. She will be admitted for conservative care to the lumbar spine. As soon as she feels better she will be followed as an outpatient.

George Crane

GEORGE CRANE, M.D.

FORM NO.: 23e MA

Exhibit 4

MACON GENERAL HOSPITAL
MACON, GEORGIA

DISCHARGE SUMMARY

PATIENT: Fisher, Julie

HOSPITAL #: 483-6290

PHYSICIAN: Crane

ADMITTED: 6-10-YR-1

DISCHARGED: 6-18-YR-1

DISCHARGE DIAGNOSIS: Low back strain

HISTORY:

This is a twenty-three year-old female who was involved in a fall a few years back which was the onset of low back discomfort which she has had since then. She was admitted through the emergency room by the emergency room physician when he felt that she was in severe pain on presentation on the evening of admission. She seemed to have several hysterical complaints on admission. She continued to be demanding and manipulative throughout admission.

HOSPITAL COURSE:

Electromyogram was performed which was negative during this hospitalization. However, she did respond to some bed rest and she was discharged to be followed as an outpatient.

CONDITION ON DISCHARGE:

Good. Patient stated she was nearly asymptomatic. Prognosis good for full recovery.

George Crane
_____
GEORGE CRANE, M.D.

FORM NO.: 15m E

Medical Terms

asymptomatic: without symptoms

auscultation: listening for sounds produced in the body cavities particularly the chest in order to detect an abnormal condition

bilaterally: affecting two side of the body

cardiomegaly: hypertrophy of the heart

CAT scan: (computerized tomography) development of an image from multiple x-rays at varying levels translated through computer on video

disc herniation: an intervertebral disk in which the center of the disc has protruded past the ligamentous tissue that connects the adjacent vertebrae. It may impinge on spinal nerves and produce mild to severe symptoms.

dorsiflexion: the act of bending or flexion toward the dorsum or upwards (opposite of plantar flexion)

electromyogram: a graphic record of the contraction of a muscle as a result of electrical stimulation

extensor hallucis longus: a muscle group in the anterior tibia-fibular region of the leg

flexion: the act of bending in contrast to extending

functional overlay: large psychological component to their complaints (not malingering)

hypesthesia: impairment of sensitivity to touch and pain

hyperesthesia: unusual sensitivity or increase in sensitivity to sensory stimuli due to nerve pathology

iliolumbar area: the area between the ilium and the lumbar process

ilium: the flank -- one of the pelvic bones

lateral: pertaining to the side

lumbar spine: five bones of the spinal column between the sacrum and thoracic vertebrae (the lower back)

organomegaly: enlargement of an organ

peroneal: concerning the fibular area

plantar flexion: contraction of the toes in an downward direction upon irritation of the sole

postero-superior:	located behind and above a part
posterolateral:	located behind and at the side of a part
quadriceps:	large group of muscles on the anterior (front) of the thigh that permit the knee to lock upon standing
q.i.d.:	four times a day
spine:	The spine is a flexible column formed of a series of bones called vertebrae (from vertere, to turn).

spine (continued):

The vertebrae are thirty-three in number, and have received the names cervical, dorsal, lumbar, sacral, and coccygeal, according to the position which they occupy; seven being found in the cervical region, twelve in the dorsal, five in the lumbar, five in the sacral, and four in the coccygeal.

The vertebrae in the upper three regions of the spine are separate throughout the whole of life; but those found in the sacral and coccygeal regions are in the adult firmly united, so as to form two bones -- five entering into the formation of the upper bone or sacrum, and four into the terminal bone of the spine or coccyx.

The bodies of the vertebrae are piled one upon the other, forming a strong pillar for the support of the cranium and trunk; the arches forming a hollow cylinder behind the bodies for protection of the spinal cord. The different vertebrae are connected together by means of the articular processes and the intervertebral fibro-cartilages; while the transverse and spinous processes serve as levers for the attachment of muscles which move the different parts of the spine. Lastly, between each pair of vertebrae apertures exist through which the spinal nerves pass from the cord. Each of these constituent parts must now be separately examined.

supine:	lying on the back with the face upward
t.i.d.:	three times a day

Exhibit — Planes of the Body

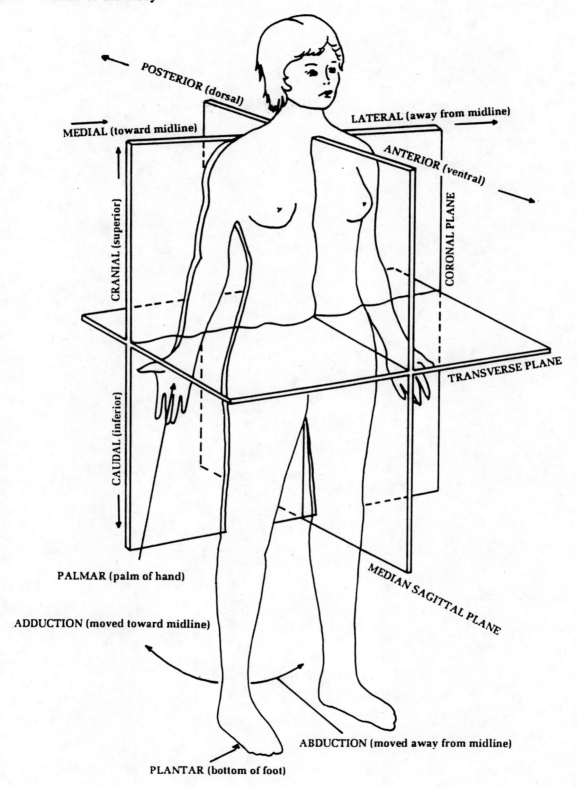

PLANES OF THE BODY

Exhibit — Vertebral Column

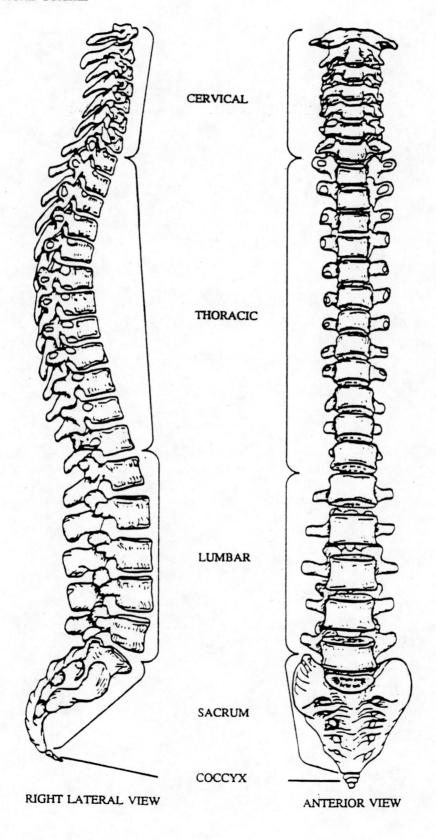

CERVICAL

THORACIC

LUMBAR

SACRUM

COCCYX

RIGHT LATERAL VIEW

ANTERIOR VIEW

JURY INSTRUCTIONS*

Closing Instruction 1
Issues in the Case

The plaintiff claims that she was injured and sustained damage as a result of the negligent conduct of the defendant. The plaintiff has burden of proving her claims.

Closing Instruction 2
Negligence

The legal term negligence, otherwise known as carelessness, is the absence of the ordinary care which a reasonable, prudent person would exercise in the circumstances here presented. Negligent conduct may consist either an act or an omission to act when there is a duty to do so. In other words, negligence is the failure to do something which a reasonably careful person would do, or the doing of something which a reasonably careful person would not do, in light of all the surrounding circumstances established by the evidence in this case. It is for you to determine how a reasonably careful person would act in those circumstances.

I further instruct you that if you find that the defendant violated the Uniform Building Code of the City of Nita, then you may consider such as evidence that the defendant was negligent, if you find that the code violation was a legal cause of plaintiff's injuries.

Closing Instruction 3
Ordinary Care

Ordinary care is the care a reasonably careful person would use under the circumstances presented in this case. It is the duty of every corporation to use ordinary care not only for the safety of its own employees and protection of its property, but also to avoid injury to others. What constitutes ordinary care varies according to the particular circumstances and conditions existing then and there. The amount of care required by the law must be in keeping with the degree of danger involved.

Closing Instruction 4
Duty of Owner of Premises

The owner of premises is under a duty to exercise ordinary care in the management of such premises in order to avoid exposing persons thereon to an unreasonable risk of harm. A failure to fulfill this duty would be negligence.

---

*These proposed instructions are those applicable to this case only. For general instructions, see those set forth after these instructions.

Owners' Liability

In determining if the defendant owner of the premises exercised ordinary care in the management of the premises, you should consider all the surrounding circumstances shown by the evidence, including but not limited to the following:

1. Was the condition of the premises reasonably safe for use for the purposes for which such premises were intended to be used?

2. Were the active operations on the premises conducted with ordinary care?

3. Should the condition which created any risk of harm have been known to a corporation exercising ordinary care under the same or similar circumstances?

4. Would a reasonably prudent corporation under the same or similar circumstances have expected the plaintiff to recognize the risk of the harm and the magnitude thereof and to avoid it?

5. Did the defendant give any warning of a risk of harm as to the condition of the premises or the active operation thereon?

Closing Instruction 5
Unreasonable Risk or Harm Defined

In determining whether any act or omission of the defendant constituted an unreasonable risk of harm, you should consider all of the surrounding circumstances shown by the evidence, including but not limited to the following:

1. Was the risk of harm one which a reasonably careful person should anticipate at all or would commonly disregard?

2. How serious were the possible consequences from the risk?

3. What was the utility, beneficial purpose, or usefulness of such act or omission of the defendant, or of the particular manner in which such act was done?

4. What alternative courses were open to the person responsible for the act or condition?

Closing Instruction 6
Did Plaintiff Exercise Ordinary Care to Avoid Injury to Herself?

If you find that the defendant did not exercise ordinary care in the management of its property to avoid injury to the plaintiff, then in determining if plaintiff exercised ordinary care to avoid injury to herself, you should consider all the surrounding circumstances shown by the evidence, including but not limited to the following matters:

1. Did the plaintiff know the condition of the premises before being injured, and if she had such knowledge, did she exercise ordinary care to avoid injury to herself?

2. Would a reasonably careful person in the plaintiff's position have realized and avoided the danger created by the condition of the premises or the activities being carried on which caused plaintiff's injuries?

Closing Instruction 7
Legal Cause

You must determine if either of the parties' actions were negligent, and if so, whether that negligence was the legal cause of the accident. Legal cause means the negligent conduct must have been a substantial factor in bringing about the injury to the plaintiff. This is what the law recognizes as legal cause. A substantial factor is an actual, real factor, although the result may be unusual or unexpected, but it is not an imaginary or fanciful factor nor a factor having no connection with the accident.

Closing Instruction 8
Comparative Negligence

If you find that one or more of the parties are negligent and that their negligence was the legal cause of the injuries to the plaintiff, it will be your responsibility to apportion the causal negligence of the parties. If you find that the plaintiff was causally negligent, this will not bar her recovery unless her causal negligence is greater than the causal negligence of the defendant against whom recovery is sought.

Closing Instruction 9
Damages

If you find that the plaintiff was injured as a result of the defendant's negligence then you must assess her damages.

To assess any actual damages, you must find from a preponderance of the evidence that the plaintiff sustained actual damages as a proximate result of the negligence of the defendant.

To the extent that any actual damages have been so established by the evidence, you shall assess, as the plaintiff's actual damages, an amount that will fairly and justly compensate her for:

1. Any reasonable expenses she may have incurred for medical expenses;

2. Any loss of past and future earnings she may have sustained;

3. Any pain and suffering, physical discomfort, or inconveniences she may have sustained; and

4. Any physical illness or injury she may have sustained.

NITA
GENERAL JURY INSTRUCTIONS

The following jury instructions are intended for use with any of the files contained in these materials regardless of whether the trial is in Nita state court or in federal court. In addition, each of the files contains special instructions dealing with the law applicable in the particular case. The instructions set forth here state general principles that may be applicable in any of the cases and may be used at the discretion of the trial judge.*

PART I
PRELIMINARY INSTRUCTIONS
GIVEN PRIOR TO THE EVIDENCE
(For Civil or Criminal Cases)

Nita Instruction 01:01 — Introduction

You have been selected as jurors and have taken an oath to well and truly try this cause. This trial will last one day.

During the progress of the trial there will be periods of time when the Court recesses. During those periods of time, you must not talk about this case among yourselves or with anyone else.

During the trial, do not talk to any of the parties, their lawyers or any of the witnesses.

If any attempt is made by anyone to talk to you concerning the matters here under consideration, you should immediately report that fact to the Court.

You should keep an open mind. You should not form or express an opinion during the trial and should reach no conclusion in this case until you have heard all of the evidence, the arguments of counsel, and the final instructions as to the law that will be given to you by the Court.

Nita Instruction 01:02 — Conduct of the Trial

First, the attorneys will have an opportunity to make opening statements. These statements are not evidence and should be considered only as a preview of what the attorneys expect the evidence will be.

---

*The instructions contained in this section are borrowed or adapted from a number of sources including California, Illinois, Indiana, Washington, and Colorado pattern jury instructions.

Following the opening statements, witnesses will be called to testify. They will be placed under oath and questioned by the attorneys. Documents and other tangible exhibits may also be received as evidence. If an exhibit is given to you to examine, you should examine it carefully, individually, and without any comment.

It is counsel's right and duty to object when testimony or other evidence is being offered that he or she believes is not admissible.

When the Court sustains an objection to a question, the jurors must disregard the question and the answer, if one has been given, and draw no inference from the question or answer or speculate as to what the witness would have said if permitted to answer. Jurors must also disregard evidence stricken from the record.

When the Court sustains an objection to any evidence the jurors must disregard that evidence.

When the Court overrules an objection to any evidence, the jurors must not give that evidence any more weight than if the objection had not been made.

When the evidence is completed, the attorneys will make final statements. These final statements are not evidence but are given to assist you in evaluating the evidence. The attorneys are also permitted to argue in an attempt to persuade you to a particular verdict. You may accept or reject those arguments as you see fit.

Finally, just before you retire to consider your verdict, I will give you further instructions on the law that applies to this case.

PART II
FINAL INSTRUCTIONS
GENERAL PRINCIPLES

General Instructions for Both Civil and Criminal Cases

Nita Instruction 1:01 — Introduction

Members of the jury, the evidence and arguments in this case have been completed, and I will now instruct you as to the law.

The law applicable to this case is stated in these instructions and it is your duty to follow all of them. You must not single out certain instructions and disregard others.

It is your duty to determine the facts, and to determine them only from the evidence in this case. You are to apply the law to the facts and in this way decide the case. You must not be governed or influenced by sympathy or prejudice for or against any party in this case. Your verdict must be based on evidence and not upon speculation, guess, or conjecture.

From time to time the court has ruled on the admissibility of evidence. You must not concern yourselves with the reasons for these rulings. You should disregard questions and exhibits that were withdrawn or to which objections were sustained.

You should also disregard testimony and exhibits that the court has refused or stricken.

The evidence that you should consider consists only of the witness's testimonies and the exhibits the court has received.

Any evidence that was received for a limited purpose should not be considered by you for any other purpose.

You should consider all the evidence in the light of your own observations and experiences in life.

Neither by these instructions nor by any ruling or remark that I have made do I mean to indicate any opinion as to the facts or as to what your verdict should be.

Nita Instruction 1:02 — Opening Statements and Closing Arguments

Opening statements are made by the attorneys to acquaint you with the facts they expect to prove. Closing arguments are made by the attorneys to discuss the facts and circumstances in the case, and should be confined to the evidence and to reasonable inferences to be drawn therefrom. Neither opening statements nor closing arguments are evidence, and any statement or argument made by the attorneys that is not based on the evidence should be disregarded.

Nita Instruction 1:03 — Credibility of Witnesses

You are the sole judges of the credibility of the witnesses and of the weight to be given to the testimony of each witness. In determining what credit is to be given any witness, you may take into account his ability and opportunity to observe; his manner and appearance while testifying; any interest, bias, or prejudice he may have; the reasonableness of his testimony considered in the light of all the evidence; and any other factors that bear on the believability and weight of the witness's testimony.

Nita Instruction 1:04 — Expert Witnesses

You have heard evidence in this case from witnesses who testified as experts. The law allows experts to express an opinion on subjects involving their special knowledge, training and skill, experience, or research. While their opinions are allowed to be given, it is entirely within the province of the jury to determine what weight shall be given their testimony. Jurors are not bound by the testimony of experts; their testimony is to be weighed as that of any other witness.

Nita Instruction 1:05 — Direct and Circumstantial Evidence

The law recognizes two kinds of evidence: direct and circumstantial. Direct evidence proves a fact directly; that is, the evidence by itself, if true, establishes the fact. Circumstantial evidence is the proof of facts or circumstances that give rise to a reasonable inference of other facts; that is, circumstantial evidence proves a fact indirectly in that it follows from other facts or circumstances according to common experience and observations in life. An eyewitness is a common example of direct evidence, while human footprints are circumstantial evidence that a person was present.

The law makes no distinction between direct and circumstantial evidence as to the degree or amount of proof required, and each should be considered according to whatever weight or value it may have. All of the evidence should be considered and evaluated by you in arriving at your verdict.

Nita Instruction 1:06 — Concluding Instruction

The Court did not in any way and does not by these instructions give or intimate any opinions as to what has or has not been proven in the case, or as to what are or are not the facts of the case.

No one of these instructions states all of the law applicable, but all of them must be taken, read, and considered together as they are connected with and related to each other as a whole.

You must not be concerned with the wisdom of any rule of law. Regardless of any opinions you may have as to what the law ought to be, it would be a violation of your sworn duty to base a verdict upon any other view of the law than that given in the instructions of the court.

General Instructions for Civil Cases Only

Nita Instruction 2:01 — Burden of Proof

When I say that a party has the burden of proof on any issue, or use the expression "if you find," "if you decide," or "by a preponderance of the evidence," I mean that you must be persuaded from a consideration of all the evidence in the case that the issue in question is more probably true than not true. Any findings of fact you make must be based on probabilities, not possibilities. It may not be based on surmise, speculation, or conjecture.

Nita Instruction 2:02 — Corporate Party

One (Both) of the parties in this case is a corporation (are corporations), and it is (they are) entitled to the same fair treatment as an individual would be entitled to under like circumstances, and you should decide the case with the same impartiality you would use in deciding a case between individuals.

IN THE CIRCUIT COURT OF
DARROW COUNTY, NITA
CIVIL DIVISION

JULIE FISHER,　　　　　　　　)
　　　Plaintiff,　　　　　　　)
　　　　　　　　　　　　　　　)　　　CIVIL ACTION
　　　v.　　　　　　　　　　　)　　　CA 85-0172
　　　　　　　　　　　　　　　)
YANKEE DOODLE CORPORATION　　)
　　　Defendant.　　　　　　　)

SPECIAL INTERROGATORY VERDICT FORM
(LIABILITY ONLY)

We the Jury, after careful and thoughtful deliberations, find the following to be true:

1. Was the defendant, Yankee Doodle Corporation, negligent?

　　　_____　　_____
　　　　YES　　　　　NO

If the answer to Interrogatory No. 1 was "Yes," answer the following Interrogatory:

2. Was the negligence of the defendant, Yankee Doodle Corporation, a legal cause of the plaintiff's injuries?

　　　_____　　_____
　　　　YES　　　　　NO

3. Was the plaintiff, Julie Fisher, negligent?

　　　_____　　_____
　　　　YES　　　　　NO

If your answer to Interrogatory No. 3 was "Yes," answer the following interrogatory:

4. Was the negligent conduct of the plaintiff, Julie Fisher, a legal cause of her injuries?

　　　_____　　_____
　　　　YES　　　　　NO

If your answer Interrogatory Nos. 2 or 4 was "Yes," then you *must* answer the following Interrogatory. In other words, if you determine that both the Yankee Doodle Corporation and Julie Fisher were negligent *and* you determine their negligence was a legal cause of the plaintiff's injuries, then you must assign a percentage of 100% to each cause. If you find there was only one party who was negligent *and* a legal cause of the plaintiff's injuries, you must assign that party as 100% at fault.

5.   Yankee Doodle Corporation,   _____%
       Defendant

       Julie Fisher,   _____%
       Plaintiff

_____
Jury Foreperson

IN THE CIRCUIT COURT OF
DARROW COUNTY, NITA
CIVIL DIVISION

JULIE FISHER,   )
    Plaintiff,   )
)   CIVIL ACTION
    v.   )   CA 85-0172
)
YANKEE DOODLE CORPORATION   )
    Defendant.   )

SPECIAL INTERROGATORY VERDICT FORM
(LIABILITY AND DAMAGES)

We the Jury, after careful and thoughtful deliberations, find the
following to be true:

1.   Was the defendant, Yankee Doodle Corporation, negligent?

               _____   _____
               YES   NO

If the answer to Interrogatory No. 1 was "Yes," answer the
following Interrogatory:

2.   Was the negligence of the defendant, Yankee Doodle
    Corporation, a legal cause of the plaintiff's injuries?

               _____   _____
               YES   NO

3.   Was the plaintiff, Julie Fisher, negligent?

               _____   _____
               YES   NO

If your answer to Interrogatory No. 3 was "Yes," answer the
following interrogatory:

4.   Was the negligent conduct of the plaintiff, Julie Fisher, a
    legal cause of her injuries?

               _____   _____
               YES   NO

If your answer Interrogatory Nos. 2 or 4 was "Yes," then you *must* answer the following Interrogatory. In other words, if you determine that both the Yankee Doodle Corporation and Julie Fisher were negligent *and* you determine their negligence was a legal cause of the plaintiff's injuries, then you must assign a percentage of 100% to each cause. If you find there was only one party who was negligent *and* a legal cause of the plaintiff's injuries, you must assign that party as 100% at fault.

5.   Yankee Doodle Corporation,   _____%
     Defendant

     Julie Fisher,   _____%
     Plaintiff

6.   The plaintiff, Julie Fisher, has sustained fair and
     reasonable damages in the amount of: $_____.

     _____
     Jury Foreperson